The Abortion Battle

Looking at Both Sides

Felicia Lowenstein

—Issues in Focus—

ENSLOW PUBLISHERS, INC.

44 Fadem Road
Box 699
Springfield, N.J. 07081
U.S.A.

P.O. Box 38
Aldershot
Hants GU12 6BP
U.K.

For my father, who taught me the love of writing.

Library of Congress Cataloging-in-Publication Data

Lowenstein, Felicia.
    The abortion battle: looking at both sides / by Felicia Lowenstein.
        p. cm. — (Issues in Focus)
    Includes bibliographical references and index.
    ISBN 0-89490-724-7
    1. Abortion—Juvenile literature. 2. Pro-life movement— Juvenile literature.
    3. Pro-choice movement—Juvenile literature.
    I. Title. II. Series: Issues in focus (Hillside, N.J.)
    HQ767.L69   1996
    363.4'6—dc20   95-42448
                                     CIP
                                     AC

Printed in the United States of America

10 9 8 7 6 5 4 3 2 1

Cover Photo: AP/Wide World Photos

Photo Credits: AP/Wide World Photos, pp. 6, 21, 25, 30, 33, 38, 43, 49, 56,
76, 81, 89, 104; Courtesy of Karen Bell, pp. 62, 67; NARAL/New York, p. 12;
Planned Parenthood Federation of America/Scott Newton, p. 97.

Contents

Acknowledgments

I wish to gratefully acknowledge the people who helped to make this book possible: Ken and Bernice Rappoport for their research and editing skills and personal support; Debby Lowenstein and Sheri Magerkurth for their invaluable interview connections and ongoing support; Dixie Patterson and Marie Tasy who opened their doors wide with offers of assistance; the young women I interviewed who took time out of their busy schedules to speak with me; and my wonderful husband, David Lowenstein, for supporting me every step of the way in spite of the personal sacrifices he had to make to do so.

1

The Decision

Kiri* was scared. No, she was absolutely terrified. She had gone to an innocent slumber party and had done something dumb.[1]

It all started when she and her friends were drinking. Everyone was having a good time. And Kiri met a terrific guy. She knew his name but not much else. He convinced her to have sex with him.

She found out she was pregnant . . . at age sixteen.

Should she tell the boy who got her pregnant? Should she tell her parents? And then, *what* should she tell her parents? What would they think of her? What would her friends think?

* Not her real name.

5

Protestors representing both sides of the abortion issue demonstrate in front of Erie Medical Center in Buffalo, New York.

Wasn't there a way she could make the whole thing disappear? An abortion, she thought, would take care of it. Kiri had always thought she would never be able to do that. But then again, it would be such an easy way out. *Nobody* would ever have to know.

Maybe she should have the baby. Then, she could keep it and become a mother. She could do that. Or she could give the baby up for adoption and get back to her normal teenage life.

Kiri wrestled with her decision. She could not yet come to grips with the fact she really was pregnant. Did that mean she actually was going to have a baby? It did not seem possible. She did not want to accept it.

Kiri had plans and dreams. She hoped to go to college. How would a baby affect her life? Would an abortion be a better choice?

So now, Kiri was just plain scared. She knew she had a difficult decision to make, and she wanted to make the right one. She wondered what the right decision was. Pro-life groups (those opposed to abortion) and pro-choice groups (those who feel it is a woman's fundamental human right to choose when or whether to have a child) would have very different ideas.

2

What Is Abortion?
Opposing Viewponts

Imagine it is you, and not Kiri, who is pregnant. You will have to make this difficult decision. Should you have the baby? Should you get an abortion?

What exactly is abortion anyway? It is not a silly question. Depending on whom you ask, you will get different answers. The dictionary defines abortion as the termination of a pregnancy after, accompanied by, resulting in, or closely followed by the death of the embryo or fetus.[1] (Fetus is a word often used to describe human offspring before birth.)

Some people, however, including many members of the Catholic Church, say various methods of birth control are the same as abortion.

Now, remember, you are the one who is pregnant. To become pregnant, you already have had sex with a man (perhaps your boyfriend). His sperm swam up into your uterus. The sperm united with an egg there. The sperm and egg came together in a process known as fertilization. This fertilized cell (sperm and egg) in your body is called a zygote. The zygote has a complete blueprint—or plan—to make a human being. Let's look at each of your choices. You could decide to have the baby and raise it, you could decide to have the baby and give it up for adoption, or you could decide to have an abortion.

Having the Baby

Suppose you decide to have the baby. Your body will follow a natural process for about nine months.

A week after fertilization, the cell in your body has already turned into several hundred cells called a blastocyst. The blastocyst floats out of the narrow tube and attaches itself to the side of your uterus. It sends chemical signals that you are pregnant.

After a month, the blastocyst becomes an embryo with three layers. The outside layer creates skin, hair, brain, and nerves. The middle layer builds muscles, bones, a heart, kidneys, veins, and reproductive organs. The inside layer makes the lungs, stomach, and intestines. If you were able to look inside your uterus at the embryo, you would notice the beginnings of arms and legs.

At two months, the embryo officially becomes a fetus. The fetus gets arms and legs, fingers and toes, and a neck and ears. Its head is much bigger than the rest of its body.

At three months, its body grows to catch up with its head. The fetus also grows fingernails, toenails, eyelids, and sex organs.

At six months, the fetus weighs about two to three pounds and measures nine to ten inches from its head to its rear end. It probably could survive outside of your uterus, if it had expert care.

The fetus continues developing until it is ready to be born. At that time, if all goes well, it will have turned upside down so it may come out head first. You will know the fetus is ready when you feel the cramps which are the contractions of the uterus. As the cramps become closer together, and more painful, the fetus is on its way out into the world. You will hear the baby's cry when the doctor delivers it and hits it on its bottom.

This is the story of a traditional birth. At this point, you could either decide to keep the baby and raise your child or you might decide to give the baby up for adoption. However, what might have happened if you decided to have an abortion instead?

Having An Abortion

If you are like many women, you probably will decide within the first three months (or first trimester) of getting pregnant whether or not to have an abortion.[2] Suppose you decide to have one. You may live in a state where you do not need your parent's permission to get an abortion, and so you decide not to tell them.

Representing their side of the story, Megan (left) and Nicole Brackett demonstrate at an anti-abortion rally in Richmond, Virginia. They hold Teddy Tomorrow bears to represent all of the abortions that have been performed since 1973.

Or like nearly 80 percent of pregnant teens, you may decide to tell them.[3]

On your own, you investigate the different places that perform abortions. Many doctors advertise their services, and there are women's clinics and organizations that will counsel you and provide abortion services. You will be told about your pregnancy options—parenting, adoption, and abortion.

You make an appointment with a clinic. You visit the clinic once to take a pregnancy test. It is positive; you are definitely pregnant. The doctor or nurse looks at the inside of your uterus with a sonogram machine (similar to an X ray). The picture shows you are nine weeks pregnant. You make an appointment to have an abortion.

Later in the week, you return for your appointment. After talking with a nurse counselor, you undress in the examining room. You lie down on the exam table covered by a white paper cloth, your feet in metal stirrups.

The doctor enters and makes casual conversation with you as he or she gets ready for the procedure. The procedure begins. A long metal tool is inserted into your vagina and opens it to hold the vaginal walls apart. A local anesthetic—or painkiller—is used to numb your cervix. The opening of your cervix widens to about half-an-inch, or the width of a pen. A small tube attached to a vacuum aspirator machine—like the one dentists use to remove saliva from your mouth—is inserted. The machine sucks up the contents of the uterus. At the end, the doctor checks the walls of your uterus with a curette—a spoon-shaped instrument—to make sure everything has been removed.[4]

The whole procedure takes ten minutes. Afterward, you experience some cramps (similar to severe menstrual cramps) for about an hour. The nurse takes your blood pressure and monitors your heart rate. Both are normal. The doctor gives you a prescription for an antibiotic, and an around-the-clock emergency number to call if you have any problems. Then, you make an appointment to return in two weeks for a final checkup—to make sure the abortion is complete and there are no problems.

Methods of Abortion

The procedure just described is the most common type of abortion. Approximately 90 percent of abortions performed in the United States use this method.[5] Doctors can use two basic methods of abortion. In one method, they widen the opening of the cervix and remove the contents of the uterus, as in the above example. The other method, which is extremely rare, causes labor, so the contents of the uterus are pushed out of the woman. This is known as the induction or instillation method. The doctor gives the patient a local anesthetic, and then injects medication into the uterus to cause labor contractions. Hours later, labor begins and the fetus is removed.

The patient was lucky. In this imaginary sequence, she was in her first trimester of pregnancy, when abortions are the safest to perform. Half of all abortions happen before the fetus is two months old, and 90 percent occur before the end of the first trimester, or three months.[6] However, when a woman is in the second trimester (second three months) of pregnancy, other methods may be used. Many of these are done in a hospital, not a doctor's office or a clinic, just in case there are complications. In this country, women in their third trimester of pregnancy are not allowed to have abortions, by law, unless their health is in danger.

If you had been in your second trimester, you might have had a variation of the vacuum aspiration method. The doctor still widens the cervix and uses the vacuum aspiration machine. However, in addition, forceps are used to pull out anything too big to fit through the tube. Then, the lining of the uterus is checked as before. This process takes from ten to thirty minutes. Or the induction or installation method might be used instead to cause labor contractions.[7]

RU-486—"The Abortion Pill"

You may have also heard about a pill you can take to cause an abortion. Such a pill does exist, and while it is quite popular in Europe, it is not yet legal in the United States. The pill is known in Europe as RU-486.[8] Its official name is mifepristone, and it was invented by French Professor Etienne-Emile Baulieu. Also called the "morning-after pill" or the "French abortion pill," RU-486 is prescribed by European doctors for women who want abortions before the eighth week of pregnancy.

How does it work? Do you remember that the fertilized egg—the blastocyst—sends chemical signals to the woman that she is pregnant? The chemical signal is sent when the body produces a special hormone called progesterone. This helps the egg to stay attached to the thick lining of the uterus.

RU-486 prevents this from happening. It blocks the action of the hormone and causes the uterine lining to break away into a menstrual period. The fertilized egg is removed in the menstrual bleeding. RU-486 works alone only 65 to 80 percent of the time. Often, as a follow-up to the pill, women are given another drug, prostaglandin, to complete the process. Prostaglandin causes the contractions that expel the fertilized egg from the uterus.

RU-486 is not for everybody. It only works in the first seven to eight weeks. After that, the body produces enough progesterone to overpower the drug. Also, it is dangerous for women who smoke or have heart disease in their family to take RU-486. One woman who was a chronic smoker with heart disease died from taking RU-486. This is the only reported death so far from this drug.[9]

Women who have tried RU-486 say it feels as if they are having a painful period, with symptoms ranging from cramps, bloating, and vomiting to nausea and diarrhea. Their period is also much heavier than normal.[10]

The United States Food and Drug Administration is currently testing RU-486 with about two thousand women volunteers. If the tests show the drug is safe, it may be approved for use in the United States. Women would not be able to take the pills at home. They would have to come to a clinic or doctor's office where they are carefully watched. RU-486 will probably cost the same as a surgical abortion, because of the required doctor visits.

How much does an abortion cost? It depends, but usually during the first trimester, abortions are about $300 and the price goes up as a woman enters the second trimester. If a pregnancy is far along, the price could be as high as $2,000. Many doctors require the money up front.[12]

Who Has Abortions?

There are about 1.6 million women who have legal abortions each year in the United States.[13] They come from all religious, racial, ethnic, and socioeconomic backgrounds. Many are young and unmarried.[14] Of those 1.6 million women, about one in four are teenagers.[15] There are also many women who have illegal abortions each year. These numbers are not recorded.

Not every teenager who gets pregnant chooses abortion. Each year in the United States, about one million teenagers—or one out of ten young women aged fifteen to nineteen—become pregnant.[16] Surveys show in most cases (82 percent), teenagers do not intend to get pregnant.[17] But, each year, about half a million teenagers give birth. One out of every eight babies born in the United States will have a teenage mother.[18]

Teenage mothers are not new; in fact, there were more of them in the 1950s. Most got married after becoming pregnant, but a small number did put their babies up for adoption. Others were older teenagers, already married, who raised their babies with their husbands. Today, many teenage mothers are fifteen or sixteen, and some are as young as twelve. Unlike the 1950s, nearly 95 percent of the teenagers who give birth today decide to raise the children themselves.[19]

Becoming pregnant certainly changes your life—
especially if you are a teenager. If you choose to have the
baby, you may give up your dreams for a career, a happy
marriage, or college. You might even have a hard time
finishing high school; only half of teenage mothers
are able to do it.[20] The Children's Defense Fund, in
Washington, D.C., estimates that each year, about forty
thousand teenagers drop out of school because they are
pregnant.[21] Some try to commit suicide. Unfortunately,
because teenage mothers rarely finish their education,
they will make about half of the income that their friends
who have finished their education will earn.[22]

Not only are teenage mothers at a disadvantage, the
babies also may suffer. If a young woman denies she is
pregnant, she may not get adequate prenatal care until
late in her pregnancy. This could harm the infant, who,
as a result, may suffer from birth defects, mental problems, epilepsy, or sudden infant death syndrome.[23]

In addition, some teenage mothers hold their
babies less and don't talk to them as much. Teenagers
also don't know a lot about nutrition. Many teenage
mothers feed their children the diet they prefer for
themselves—pizza, potato chips, and other junk
food.[24] Also, the child may be neglected, rejected, or
abused by the teenage mother because the baby may
remind her of the mistake she made.

What do teenagers think about pregnancy and abortion? *People* magazine surveyed boys and girls aged
fourteen to eighteen and found these results. Overall,
65 percent of teenagers thought getting pregnant or

fathering a child was a "bad turn of events" while 26 percent thought it was good. The teenagers were nearly evenly split on the question of abortion: 52 percent thought teenage girls should have the right and 46 percent did not.[25]

Two Sides to the Story

Whether you side with those teenagers who think girls should have the right to abortion, or those who think girls should not, you can find support for your point of view. There are two sides to the abortion issue. One side calls itself "pro-choice." They believe it is a woman's fundamental human right to decide when and whether to have a child. The other side calls itself "pro-life" or "right-to-life." They believe that a fetus's right to live comes first, before the rights of the pregnant woman.

Pro-Choice

Counting national, state, and local organizations, there are hundreds of groups representing both sides of this issue. Groups on the pro-choice side include the National Abortion and Reproductive Rights Action League (NARAL), the Center for Population Options, Planned Parenthood Federation of America, the National Abortion Federation, and Choice. These organizations do such things as sponsor public education programs, testify before lawmakers in Washington, D.C., protest at rallies, provide counseling to pregnant women, and help them find safe abortion services. A majority have small paid staffs and rely on volunteers to help them do the work.

Many of the larger groups have offices in states throughout the United States.

Pro-Life

The pro-life side is structured in a similar way. Some of these groups include Human Life International, Last Harvest, National Right to Life Committee, Heartbeat International, American Victims of Abortion, and the American Life League. They also sponsor educational programs, testify before lawmakers, and counsel pregnant women. Many of these organizations help women find free pregnancy care and housing during their pregnancy. Some also coordinate adoptions of newborn babies. These groups, too, are based throughout the United States, and rely on volunteers to help them do the work.

If you would like to learn more about these and other groups, consult the Where to Go for Help section of this book, under the Pro-Life Groups and the Pro-Choice Groups headings. You may also talk with your local reference librarian for a more complete list.

The pro-choice and pro-life forces have very different views on abortion.

Who is right? You will have to decide for yourself. Your view on abortion is a distinctly personal choice. No one can make it for you. You will have to learn as much as you can about the issue, and then decide what feels right to you. The answer you find will be the right choice for you now. As you grow older, you may strengthen your views or even change your opinion. That

Police carry an Operation Rescue volunteer away from a clinic in
Amherst, New York.

is because your view on abortion is a reflection of your feelings and experiences over time. The Supreme Court decided in its landmark 1973 decision of the *Roe* v. *Wade* case to make abortion a legal option for all women (through their second trimester of pregnancy). Whether or not you agree with that decision is something only you can decide.

3

From Ancient Times
to Current Law

In 1969, a young woman would change the history of abortion laws in the United States. At twenty-one years old, Norma McCorvey already had been married, divorced, and had a five-year-old daughter. Now, she was pregnant again.

She did not want to have the baby. She had no place to live . . . no job. She could not even afford to raise her own daughter—who was living in Arkansas with McCorvey's mother and stepfather. How could she possibly care for another baby?[1]

McCorvey tried to find someone who would perform an abortion. According to an 1857 state law, Texas did not allow abortions—unless a woman's life was in danger.[2] McCorvey was perfectly healthy and in no physical danger from childbirth; and therefore she could not have a legal abortion in Texas.

She explored other options. She did not have the money to travel to another state, though. Finally, McCorvey gave up. She contacted a lawyer about putting her unborn baby up for adoption.

That was her lucky break. The lawyer listened to her story and asked her to meet with some other lawyers who might be interested in her case. McCorvey did not know why, but she soon found out.

The lawyers McCorvey met were twenty-six-year-old Linda Coffee and twenty-three-year-old Sarah Weddington. The women were looking for a pregnant woman to help them change the abortion law in Texas by filing a lawsuit—or formal complaint—against the state law. Did McCorvey want to be that person?

After many meetings with the lawyers, McCorvey finally agreed to file the suit. This started a turn of events that would make abortions legal in every state in the United States. In fact, it would undo laws created just about a hundred years earlier.[3]

Abortions used to be legal, not only in the United States but all over the world. Centuries ago, not only were abortions legal, they were common. Abortion is *not* a new medical procedure invented in this century. It has been used for literally thousands of years.

Early History

Perhaps the first abortions were performed in ancient Greece and Rome. There, women used herbs to create

Sarah Weddington, one of Norma McCorvey's lawyers, holds a copy of the Supreme Court's *Roe* v. *Wade* decision. The landmark decision legalized abortions in the United States.

contractions and speed up labor when giving birth. They discovered these same herbs could be used early in pregnancy to abort a fetus. Herbs continued to be popular throughout the centuries. However, it was hard to mix the same concentrations of herbs each time, and so some women died from an overdose, or did not drink enough to abort the fetus.[4]

Views on abortion changed over time. Ancient societies like Assyria had the same punishment for abortion as they did for murder. Some of the ancient Greeks said abortion was wrong because the embryo was the same as the future child. Another group of Greeks thought the embryo was not a person, so abortion was not murder. Greek philosopher Aristotle thought abortion should be used for population control.[5]

In the 1700s, women used ergot, a substance made from rotten rye and wheat, to induce abortion. They also used parsley—which sometimes contained a chemical called apiol. Both methods were effective in causing abortions.[6]

In the 1800s, women caused abortions by drinking poisons such as arsenic, lead, and phosphorus. Many women ended up poisoning themselves instead, and died. In the second half of the 1800s, surgery was introduced as a new way to perform abortions.[7]

In the 1900s, drugs—such as quinine—were used to abort the fetus. As with poisons, large doses of drugs sometimes killed the women instead. Later in the century, a suction abortion (using a vacuum instrument like the one described in Chapter 2) was invented.[8]

Throughout history, women have had abortions, whether legal or not—even if it meant risking their lives with unsafe methods. Over time, the abortion controversy grew.

Religion and Abortion

Different religions took sides. Many mainstream religions became pro-choice. They did not want their government to make decisions about a personal choice like pregnancy.[9]

Most Protestant, Jewish, or Muslim religions in the United States support legalized abortion in cases of violent crime (rape and incest) and when the woman's life is in danger. Some denominations of these religions accept abortion for broader reasons.

The Religious Coalition for Reproductive Choice, a pro-choice organization, lists a variety of different religions that have long been pro-choice. These include Protestant denominations, such as The United Church of Christ, the Episcopal Church, the Presbyterian Church (United States), and the United Methodists. The organization also mentions the Unitarian Universalists, the United Synagogue of Conservative Judaism, and the Union of American Hebrew Congregations, all of which support the right to choose abortion as an alternative.[10]

The one religious organization which has consistently taken a strong stand against abortion is the Catholic Church. In A.D. 1150, the church accepted early abortions, only declaring it murder when a male embryo was forty days old or a female embryo was eighty days old. In many cases, abortions were viewed as murder after the time "quickening"—or movement from the embryo—was felt. In the 1800s, the Catholic Church took its firm stand on abortion as murder from the time of conception.[11]

While abortion is often a hot topic in religious beliefs, it is not specifically mentioned in, nor governed by, the Bible. However, people on both sides of the issue will cite passages from the Bible to support their views. For example, people who are pro-choice may quote a passage about life beginning when a child takes a breath. People on the other side may quote a passage that says God is aware of us in the womb.

There were no abortion laws at all in the United States until the 1800s. Connecticut and New York were the first two states to pass laws against abortions. By 1900, every state had outlawed abortion unless the abortion was performed to save the life of the pregnant woman.[12]

While feminists, women who actively support women's rights, are often associated with the right to have an abortion, many early feminists actually helped to pass laws *against* abortion. These early feminists disagreed with abortion, not because it was unsafe, but rather because they felt it was unjust. Noted feminist Susan B. Anthony called abortion "child-murder." Her friend and fellow feminist Elizabeth Cady Stanton thought abortion was the same as infanticide—killing infants. In a letter to a friend, Stanton wrote in 1873,

"When we consider that women are treated as property, it is degrading to women that we should treat our children as property to be disposed of as we see fit."[13] In protest, Stanton and Anthony's newspaper, *The Revolution,* refused to print advertisements for medicines causing abortions.

Changing Laws

In the 1960s, the American Medical Association approved abortions in certain cases—to protect the woman's physical and mental health, in the case of rape, and if the fetus was abnormal. In 1964, women got legal abortions after a German measles epidemic, because the disease could have harmed the fetus, causing birth defects. At this time, many states began to change their abortion laws. These included Alaska, Colorado, Hawaii, New York, and Washington.

Roe v. *Wade*

Several years later, Norma McCorvey was meeting with her lawyers. Her lawyers persuaded some other people to join McCorvey in filing the suit. These included a married couple who wanted an abortion and a doctor who performed abortions in Texas.

They filed the lawsuit against Henry Wade, the district attorney in Dallas, Texas. He was responsible for enforcing the Texas law. The judge named McCorvey and the group "Jane Roe"—a false name to be used to protect their privacy when anyone talked

Celebrities demonstrate for choice. The line includes (left to right) Glenn Close, Jane Fonda, Marlo Thomas, Whoopi Goldberg, and Cybill Shepherd. Although many feminists today are seen as pro-choice advocates, many early feminists helped pass laws against abortion.

about their side of the case. Their case was known as *Roe* versus (against) *Wade* or *Roe* v. *Wade.*

Three federal district court judges heard the case. There seemed to be good arguments on both sides. How would they ever make a decision? Lawyers Coffee and Weddington tried to relax. They had done the best job they could. They would learn the decision in a few weeks, when it was typed and distributed by the clerk's office.

The decision was released almost a month later in a thirteen-page paper. The judges had ruled in favor of Jane Roe. But, the ruling did not order the state to stop enforcing its abortion law. This meant other women in Texas would still have problems getting an abortion.

The lawyers filed an appeal. An appeal takes the case to another, higher-level court for a decision. They wanted to stop the state from enforcing its abortion law. Coffee and Weddington approached McCorvey, who had just had her baby and was trying to decide whether she should give it up for adoption. McCorvey filed the appeal. Even if it was too late for her to get an abortion, maybe other young women like her would be able to get one.[14]

This time, *Roe* v. *Wade* was heard by the highest court in America, the United States Supreme Court in Washington, D.C. The Supreme Court Justices met in early December 1971, to hear arguments in the case. The Justices heard both sides. It was a difficult decision. McCorvey's lawyers argued their point—the government should not be able to interfere with personal decisions.

People had a right to privacy. This was a right under the Fourteenth Amendment to the United States Constitution. Abortion is a personal decision. Was that enough to win the case?

On the other hand, Henry Wade's lawyers argued that abortion is murder. Abortions kill babies. If the mother's life is endangered by the fetus, then abortion is understandable. But, the lawyers argued, McCorvey's life was not endangered by the fetus. She would be killing a human life which would most likely become a healthy baby.

Some of the Justices agreed with Norma McCorvey's lawyers. Others agreed with Henry Wade's lawyers. After hours and hours of arguing, they agreed to decide the case at another time.

The Supreme Court Justices met again in October 1972, and then again months later. Finally, they were ready to announce their decision. Reporters crowded into the courtroom that Monday, January 22, 1973.

Supreme Court Justice Blackmun stepped forward to read the decision. "A state criminal abortion statute of the current Texas type . . . is violative of . . . the 14th Amendment."[15] The onlookers listened carefully. He was supporting Roe—government should not interfere with personal decisions. The Supreme Court had ruled in favor of Jane Roe. For the first time in history, the Supreme Court had overturned a state's abortion law. The decision to have an abortion was left to a woman and her doctor during the first trimester of pregnancy. During the second trimester, a state

Pictured ten years after arguing *Roe* v. *Wade*, attorney Linda Coffee shows pages in a law book that discuss the Supreme Court's decision to legalize abortion.

could only prevent an abortion to protect the pregnant woman's health.[16]

When people heard the decision, many chose sides. Mothers disagreed with daughters, husbands with wives. Friends argued heatedly over whether the decision was right. Officials from the Catholic Church voiced their disapproval. Women's groups voiced their support. In a matter of days, the Supreme Court Justices seemed to have torn apart the country.

Following *Roe* v. *Wade*, many human life amendments were presented to Congress. Amendments, if passed, have the power to change the law. Each of these human life amendments would make abortions illegal again. Congress did not pass these, but it did pass the Right to Conscience Bill to prevent doctors and nurses from being forced to perform abortions if they did not want to do them.

The Debate Continues

In 1976, the United States Supreme Court again looked at abortion. In *Planned Parenthood of Central Missouri* v. *Danforth*, the Justices ruled that a husband's or parent's permission is not needed in order for a woman to get an abortion.[17] Later court and Congressional decisions determined government does not have to pay for abortions either.[18]

In 1981, the Supreme Court ruled on a case that would change the lives of many teenagers in the United States. In *H. L.* v. *Matheson*, the Court agreed with a Utah law requiring minors (children under eighteen) to get their parents' permission before they can get an abortion.[19] In many states, similar laws were passed requiring parental consent. (See the next chapter and the appendix for more details on parental consent laws.)

Both Sides "Speak Out"

Because the right to an abortion is a highly charged emotional issue, groups on both sides have been active in marches and protests. Traditionally, in a march or protest, people gather at a site, often in Washington, D.C., or near a court deciding on the issue or a clinic where abortions are performed. The right to march is protected under the First Amendment to the Constitution guaranteeing freedom of expression. The marchers carry signs that tell their side of the story. Sometimes there is a rally with speakers. Usually, the other side is present in smaller numbers. Many marches have been held in the past few decades.

In addition to marches, groups on both sides have made themselves known in isolated incidents. One example of a peaceful protest occurred in South Dakota in 1981.[20] Physician Buck Williams added abortion to his list of services. At his church the next Easter, someone set up a display of crosses—eight hundred of them—representing the number of abortions he had performed that year.

In another example, the Georgia Right to Life group picketed Turner Broadcasting's CNN Center in Atlanta in 1989.[21] Protesting TBS's plans to air a documentary called "Abortion for Survival," they asked TBS also to air a documentary showing their side of the issue. Their documentary, "Eclipse of Reason," was produced by Dr. Bernard Nathanson. The film shows an aborted twenty-four-week-old fetus and is a sequel to *The Silent Scream*. Instead of showing their film, Ted Turner decided to air a debate on the abortion issue following the documentary.

Operation Rescue is a pro-life organization which protests at abortion clinics. In Boston, on September 8, 1992, the members blocked the front and back doors of a clinic with cars and then locked their necks to the underside of the cars so they could not be moved. Patients entered and left the clinic via the fire escapes. It took eight hours to remove the people and open the clinic doors. That same day, at another clinic in Boston, members of this group chained themselves together in the hallway to block it.[22]

Today, Operation Rescue cannot block clinics without penalties, under the Federal Freedom of Access to Clinic Entrances Act. This act, signed by President Bill Clinton in 1994, makes it a federal crime to block access to an abortion clinic. Along these same lines, the Supreme Court ruled it is constitutional to have a thirty-six-foot buffer zone around clinics and to ban excessive noise.[23]

On the other side of the issue, more than one hundred pro-choice demonstrators gathered in Washington, D.C., on May 21, 1985. Each of these women had abortions and believed other women should have the right to do so. Sponsored by the National

Abortion and Reproductive Rights Action League (NARAL), the rally featured speakers who told about their abortion decisions. Beginning at 7 A.M., the rally lasted into the night. The women read thousands of letters from people in every state who had abortions.[24]

In addition to protesting, people who feel strongly about this issue—both pro-life and pro-choice—spend time in educational efforts. You may have seen some of the literature distributed by these groups or you may have heard someone speak on the issue. Their attitude toward the abortion issue was probably shaped by their own experiences, their religious beliefs, and what they learned about this issue from family members and friends.

For example, the National Abortion and Reproductive Rights Action League (NARAL) of New York, one of forty-one state chapters, holds an annual Pro-Choice Lobby Day in Albany, the state capital. Each year, the students attend workshops in the morning and meet with legislators in the afternoon. They communicate their feelings on such topics as abortion, parental consent laws, and sex education. Many high school age students work with organizations such as NARAL, to help them educate others about the issue.

Not everyone is calm about this issue. If you read the newspapers, you may see a number of alarming, violent acts against abortion clinics. Between 1984 and 1994, there were 153 attempted or successful bombings and fires at abortion clinics throughout the United

Abortion is an issue that affects all Americans—including teenagers. At New York/NARAL's lobby day, teenagers stand behind assemblymen and others during a press conference on choice and teen health issues in Albany, New York. The panel requested funds for school-based health clinics.

States—adding up to about $13 million in damages.[25] In 1993, forty-seven-year-old Dr. David Gunn was murdered outside of his Florida clinic, Pensacola Women's Medical Services. A year later, Floridian Michael Griffin was convicted of first-degree murder and sentenced to life in prison for that crime.

Also in 1993, an abortion physician, Dr. George Tiller, was shot. A woman was found guilty of attempted murder and sentenced to ten years in prison.

In 1993, clinics were set on fire in Corpus Christi, Texas; Bakersfield, California; and Jacksonville, Florida.

In 1994, sixty-nine-year-old Dr. John Bayard Britton was performing abortions at the only other clinic in Pensacola, Florida. (Dr. David Gunn was killed at the first clinic there.) He and his volunteer escort were both shot and killed as they left the clinic one day. The bullets wounded Dr. Britton's wife, June, who was nearby. Paul Hill, a father of three and a former Presbyterian minister, was arrested just a few minutes after the shooting.

In the trial, Hill acted as his own lawyer. He argued that killing a doctor was the "lesser evil" acceptable in order to stop the "greater evil" of allowing abortions. The jury took only twenty minutes to convict Paul Hill. The judge sentenced him to death in the electric chair.[26]

In response, New York-based Cardinal John J. O'Connor offered himself as a target to be killed instead of the next abortion doctor. In *Catholic New York*, he wrote, "If anyone has an urge to kill an abortionist, let him kill me instead. That's about as clearly as I can renounce such madness."[27]

In 1994, a man sprayed gunfire at two Boston-area abortion clinics, killing the receptionist at each and wounding five others. The clinics closed down temporarily, reopening with tougher security and metal detectors. Bernard Cardinal Law, Archbishop of Boston, called for an end to sidewalk protests outside clinics.[28] The suspect in the shootings was twenty-two-year-old John C. Salvi III from New Hampshire. He then traveled down to Norfolk, Virginia, to launch a similar attack there, and was finally caught by the police.

These acts of violence are the work of individuals or extremist pro-life groups. Many people who support pro-life views do not support their actions. Rather, they respect all human life, including that of the doctors, receptionists, and pregnant women. In a meeting on this issue, our nation's Christian religious leaders voiced their opinion in defense of the pro-life movement. They hoped the majority of peaceful pro-lifers would not be associated with these radicals.[29]

The murders of abortion doctors so angered medical students around the country that they formed a group called Medical Students for Choice. The students are trying to get medical schools to offer more courses on abortion, and they have been successful in several schools so far. Planned Parenthood of New York also started a training program on abortion for doctors. Now, the American College of Graduate Medical Education—which supervises doctors' education—is deciding whether abortion should be required for those who want to practice obstetrics and gynecology.

Today, four of the Supreme Court Justices who originally voted to legalize abortion in *Roe* v. *Wade* have since left the court. A new, more conservative court may overturn this ruling in future judgments. The legal effects would depend on the Court's basis for its decision. In *Roe* v. *Wade*, the Court did not address the question of when life begins. If a future

Court does address that question and overturns *Roe* v. *Wade* on that basis, it could mean the complete prohibition of abortion. No one can predict what will happen. The best you can do is to educate yourself about the issue and to work for what you believe is right. To help you decide, the next section gives you more information about the two sides of the abortion issue.

The Opposing Views

Now that you know about abortion and its history, think for a moment how you might feel about getting one done. Many things can affect your feelings. For example, your religion may tell you whether abortion is acceptable.

Your own experiences also can influence your opinion. Dr. Bernard Nathanson was an American gynecologist in charge of a large abortion clinic in New York City. He was strongly pro-choice. But one day, while experimenting with an aborted fetus, Dr. Nathanson saw the human element in it. He decided that what he was doing was wrong. From that moment, Dr. Nathanson became a pro-lifer. In fact, he made one of the most famous anti-abortion films called *The Silent Scream*.

Lindsay,* a freelance writer and a parent, did the reverse. She was raised in a strict Catholic environment and taught that abortion was wrong. Lindsay volunteered for pro-life groups, absolutely convinced that abortion was the wrong thing to do. It wasn't until

* Not her real name.

she had a baby that she began to change her mind. Her relationship with the child's father was on shaky ground. The baby girl was difficult to care for, and cried all the time. Lindsay was extremely depressed. There were no friends and family nearby for support. "I can't imagine anybody having to go through what I did, without being prepared for it," says Lindsay, who now talks differently about abortion. "I definitely feel that women should have the right to choose. It's such a big decision in anybody's life."[30]

As you read the ideas of both sides, compare them to your thoughts on the subject.

The Right-to-Life View

When does life begin? Well, according to many pro-lifers, life begins when the sperm fertilizes the egg. Other pro-lifers say that life begins just a few days later, when the fertilized egg implants itself in the woman's uterus. Either way, pro-lifers say that abortion is equivalent to murdering a human being—because a life is removed from its source. The egg cannot live outside the woman's uterus. Pro-life activists say that abortion destroys a basic right of a child—the right to be born.

Is there a good reason for abortion? Most pro-lifers would say no, unless perhaps the mother's life is in danger.

A major pro-life concern is that women may use abortion to replace birth control. Instead of investing in a prescription for the birth control pill, or in condoms, women may have unprotected sex. Then, they

District Attorney Henry Wade leaves the courtroom in Dallas, Texas. More than twenty years after the *Roe* v. *Wade* decision, four of the deciding Supreme Court Justices have left the court. A new, more conservative court could overrule the decision in the future.

might have abortions when they get pregnant. Pro-life groups track this by putting together statistics on repeat abortions. At the time of *Roe* v. *Wade,* about 12 percent of the abortions performed in the United States were repeat abortions. By 1983, 38.8 percent of the abortions performed were repeat abortions. In 1987, there were about 643,500 repeat abortions, with 53,250 having a fourth abortion, 17,500 having a fifth abortion, 4,400 having a sixth abortion, and another 4,400 having seven or more.[31] It is not uncommon, say pro-lifers, for women to become upset they have killed their unborn baby, and to start a "replacement" pregnancy. Therefore, the cycle just continues with no end insight.

Would women have abortions if they were illegal? Pro-lifers know they would. But, they feel these women should be punished.

Are abortions really safe for the woman? Pro-lifers say no. They believe that abortions have many negative physical and psychological effects.

The right-to-life groups believe there are many physical side effects:

1) Pelvic inflammatory disease is an infection which can follow abortion, and happens up to 30 percent of the time.

2) Abortions may damage the cervix. The muscle could be torn when it is stretched open. The womb could be punctured by the abortion instruments. This could lead to later miscarriages, bleeding during pregnancy, or premature birth.

3) Abortion prevents some women—3 to 5 percent—from getting pregnant again.

4) New pregnancies following abortions may result in increased bleeding.[32]

The right-to-life groups also talk about the psychological effects of abortion. Pro-lifers believe abortion has particularly harmful effects on teenagers.[33] The Medical College of Ohio studied how teenagers were able to cope with abortions as compared to adult women. They studied thirty-five women who had abortions as teenagers and thirty-six women who had abortions after age twenty. They found there were two factors present in teenage abortions. First, people other than the teenager had control of the abortion decision (including parents, sexual partners, or peers). Second, teenagers are less knowledgeable about the procedure and may have false ideas about it. Also, teenagers were less likely to consult a professional before making their decision. The study showed teenagers experienced greater stress during the abortion.

What about the fetus? Does the fetus feel anything during an abortion? Pro-life activists show film footage of abortions, where the fetus moves away from the abortion tools. This, they believe, is evidence that the fetus feels pain.[34] They call this a "silent scream." Pro-lifers do not want to allow a death, much less a painful one.

How old must a fetus be before it can survive outside of the woman's womb? With the medical technology we now have, a fetus probably needs to be six months—or twenty-six weeks—old before it can do so.[35]

Monte Harris Liebman, M.D., of People for Life, outlines some additional arguments against abortion in his materials. According to him, abortion deprives the community of a new life, and in many cases, prevents the formation of a family. Abortion goes against our constitutional right to life. The fetus is helpless to defend itself. Abortions encourage fetal research—dissecting unborn babies to learn more about human development.

The pro-lifers ask people to consider this. The heart of a fetus starts pumping at eighteen days after the sperm and egg come together. The brain starts working at forty days. All of a fetus's body systems are in place by the time it is two months old.[36]

At two months, the fetus sucks its thumb, as a baby does. At ten weeks, the fetus squints, moves its tongue and swallows, just like a human. At four months, the fetus has its own set of unique fingerprints—different from any living person. By seven months, the fetus is using four of its senses: seeing, hearing, taste, and touch. It knows its mother's voice, as a baby does.[37]

Pro-lifers believe this evidence shows a fetus is alive. They say it fits the definition. What is a life? According to the pro-lifers, it is a growing being that continues to make new cells. Human beings have forty-six chromosomes in every cell. So does a fetus. It is a complete being, pro-lifers claim, because nothing else will be added to it until birth. It simply will need time to develop. A fetus is not simply a piece of tissue. Pro-lifers see fetuses as unique individuals; there are no other people just like them. For these reasons, pro-lifers feel the fetus has a soul and is a person worthy of respect. They conclude that aborting a fetus is the same as murdering a person.[38]

Are there any situations in which abortion is acceptable for pro-lifers? What about rape or incest? Rape is when a woman is forced to have sex against her will. Incest is rape but by a family member (sometimes a father, brother, or uncle). Both rape and incest are violent crimes which can cause physical and psychological pain. Often, these crimes go unreported, because of embarrassment or in an effort to hide the fact they occurred.

According to the Catholic Church, the only time abortion is acceptable is when the mother would die if she were to give birth—a rare occurrence today. The Church believes a baby should be born, even in cases of rape or incest. Many, although not all, pro-lifers agree.

The first point many pro-lifers make is that a law allowing raped women to get abortions would only affect a few women—less than .1 percent of all abortions each year.[39] However, with large numbers of rapes and cases of incest going unreported, this number is misleading.

Pro-lifers believe the damage already has happened—that of the rape. An abortion will simply cause more psychological and physical harm. Even though half of the fetus is part of the rapist, half of the fetus is part of the woman, too. They believe it is in unfair to kill a being who was not responsible for the rape.[40]

Their feeling is the same for incest. In cases where abortion is chosen, pro-life activists believe an innocent baby is killed for a crime its father commits. The father, instead, should suffer. Pro-lifers believe if abortion is chosen, it helps to hide the fact that incest took place—and it might continue.[41]

What if the child has a severe genetic handicap and will not be able to lead a "normal" life? Is abortion acceptable to pro-lifers then? Dr. C. Everett Koop, M.D., former United States Surgeon General, once said that physical or mental handicaps do not necessarily go hand in hand with unhappiness. Some of the unhappiest children he has met have not had any handicaps, while some of the happiest children he has met have dealt with challenging problems.

If a pregnancy test mistakenly indicated that a fetus is healthy, and the child is born with a birth defect, is it acceptable to kill that child? No, the law would not allow it. Doing so says the child is unacceptable to live. This brings up similar situations in the past—in Hitler's Germany or American slavery—when certain people said who had the right to live. The pro-life side sees no difference between infanticide—killing infants—and abortion—killing a fetus. They say nearly 26 million unborn children in the United States have been killed by abortion since its legalization. They compare this figure to Hitler's Holocaust.[42]

What can you do if you do not want to have an abortion? One choice is to have, and raise, the child. Nearly one million children each year are born to unwed

Anti-abortionists march in Washington, D.C., on the anniversary of the *Roe* v. *Wade* decision.

mothers and half of those to unwed women under twenty.[42] Another choice is to have the baby and put it up for adoption. According to the National Council for Adoption, about twenty-five thousand babies are given up for adoption each year.[44] Pro-lifers feel adoption, or even foster care, is preferable to abortion.

The one point pro-lifers emphasize is this. Abortion is a final decision that cannot be later changed or corrected. The woman cannot get her baby back. The woman may regret her decision for the rest of her life.

Who are the people who are pro-life? Here is a snapshot view of some of the groups.

The American Life League has more than two hundred fifty thousand members throughout the country. They provide educational materials and hold meetings and training sessions. Their staff also researches statistics. The abortion issue is just one of their focuses.

Forlife is responsible for producing educational materials. For example, their materials include videotapes, films and filmstrips, plays and puppet shows, brochures, and books. They also assist other groups in producing pro-life materials.

Heartbeat International has regional contacts throughout the United States. This group provides services to pregnant women and helps with problem pregnancies. Heartbeat International also offers emotional, medical, and legal support to women who are thinking about abortion. Each year, the group compiles the World-Wide Pro-Life Emergency Pregnancy Services Directory, available to the public for a small fee.

Human Life International has five hundred thousand members, forty-two regional groups, and fifteen state groups. This group researches and educates about family planning, abortion, and sex education, among other human life issues. They have a charitable program, and award scholarships for pro-life work and leadership. Human Life International also provides speakers to talk about life issues to local organizations or groups of people who are interested.

Last Harvest has 215 local groups. In addition to providing educational materials, the group produces radio programs about abortion and provides speakers who will come to any group. Last Harvest also counsels women who have had, or may have, abortions and provides a retreat where women can recover from the aftereffects of an abortion.

The National Life Center is a central base for private pregnancy centers throughout the country. The centers are operated by volunteers who help women find alternatives to abortion. The National Life Center will put young women in touch with a center near them.

Operation Rescue is an organization that demonstrates at abortion clinics throughout the nation. Its goal is to disrupt the operation of these clinics. For example, protestors may try to persuade women not to enter the clinic or take more drastic measures such as blocking the entrance or chaining themselves in the hallways. However, the group does not approve of violence to reach its goals.

Save A Baby educates the public about the dangers of abortion through television and radio programs, speeches, and materials. The group provides maternity clothes, baby clothes, and other supplies to pregnant women who may not be able to afford them. Through volunteers, it also provides some medical care.

The Pro-Choice View

Now that you have learned a little more about the pro-life side, let's take a look at the pro-choice views. They quote United States and state law, both of which do not consider the fetus a person. The pro-choice position is based on the belief that it is a woman's fundamental human right to decide when or whether to have a child. They also believe that women should have the right to the most statistically and scientifically accurate comprehensive and unbiased information in order to make their decision.

While the pro-choice side fights for the right to have an abortion, they make the distinction between "pro-choice" and "pro-abortion." These groups want women to be *able to choose* an abortion if it is right for them. However, they do not necessarily believe abortion is the solution for everyone. That is why they prefer to be called pro-choice rather than pro-abortion.

If abortion is the right choice for a woman, she shouldn't have to worry about its safety, say pro-choicers. The procedure is perfectly safe. According to the National Abortion Federation, having an abortion in the first three months of pregnancy is safer than giving birth to a child. Women hardly ever die from legal abortions—only one in two hundred thousand. Women are seven times more likely to die from childbirth than from a legal abortion.[45]

The earlier an abortion is done, the safer it is. Pro-choicers stress the fact that most abortions—about 95 percent—are done during the first trimester. Less than one percent are done after the twentieth week, and usually only for medical reasons.[46] Many pro-choicers criticize the anti-abortion film *The Silent Scream*—showing buckets of stillborn fetuses up to six months old—as misleading. Fetuses that advanced in development would not be likely legal abortion candidates in the United States.

Unfortunately, say pro-choicers, more than 35 percent of abortions after twelve weeks are performed on teenagers. This is because teenagers may not recognize the signs of pregnancy or may become pregnant before they menstruate for the first time or before their periods are regular. They also may delay telling parents or other adults until they cannot hide it any longer. Although abortions are safe, waiting increases the risk.

Safety is important if you are choosing abortion. Here are some more pro-choice facts about the safety of this procedure.

(1) Abortion is one of the safest medical procedures available.

(2) Government studies show a pregnancy carried to term causes more complications than any legal abortion. A legal abortion during the first trimester is much safer than giving birth.

(3) Pro-choice supporters say having an abortion does not affect future pregnancies.

(4) There are no significant psychological after-effects of legal abortion. According to an American Psychiatric Association report published in *Science* magazine in 1990, legal abortion requested by the woman does not cause emotional problems or depression. Some women may feel sad or guilty at first, but not any more or less than any other personal crisis.

(5) In particular, teenagers who had abortions seem to behave more normally than others who gave birth to a baby. Teenagers who have abortions are more likely to graduate high school, go to college, and

get good jobs. However, teenagers who "have a baby when they are sixteen or younger are more likely to have another baby within two years than girls who have a baby at seventeen or eighteen years old."[47]

A woman chooses abortion for many reasons, but usually because the pregnancy at that moment is wrong for her. That doesn't mean she won't feel sad about her decision. The National Abortion Federation reports that most women who choose abortion may temporarily feel a sense of loss, but in the long run, most feel "relief" and are satisfied they made the right decision for themselves.[48]

Are abortions done for trivial reasons? Pro-choicers say no. Most people do not use abortions in place of birth control. Nor do people use it to choose a child's gender. In the United States, the only time an abortion is performed because of the gender of the fetus is when there is a gender-linked genetic disease.[49]

Are abortions painful for the fetus? Again, the pro-choice side says no. The fetus's brain is not well developed enough to feel pain during an abortion, according to the American College of Obstetricians and Gynecologists. Nor does the fetus cry out. Fetal brains have not developed the part of the brain which feels pain until after the twenty-eighth week of pregnancy. Science is still researching whether a fetus is able to feel pain. Scientists at the Harvard Medical School say the nerve connections that allow people to feel pain do start to develop at eight weeks. However, the connections are not complete until the last three months of pregnancy; therefore, scientists assume no pain is felt.[50]

Would abortions disappear if they were made illegal? Pro-choicers say no, women will still have illegal, "back-alley" abortions if they become outlawed—just as they did before *Roe* v. *Wade.* Complications from abortions were the single largest killer of women of childbearing age when abortion was illegal (1860–1973).[51] Abortions did not stop. Women just went to any available source for unsafe abortions or tried to perform their own abortions. After their illegal abortions, many went to emergency rooms with serious problems—severe bleeding, wounds to their cervix or uterus, infection, shock, and gangrene. Some of these women, and many others who did not make it to the emergency room, died as a result.

Should abortions be allowed in cases of rape and incest? Absolutely yes, say pro-choicers. There may be serious psychological effects from having a child that was the result of a horrible experience like incest or rape. Pro-choice supporters believe if the woman decides to raise the child, they say, she will have a constant reminder of the incident. Surveys have shown many people would accept abortion in cases of rape, serious birth defects, or a woman's life being at risk.[52] Medical research has not determined whether there are genetic tendencies toward sexual crimes. The child may carry some of those genes.

Planned Parenthood, a reproductive health-care provider, gives additional reasons why abortions should be legal. Legal abortions help to keep women healthy. Some women have medical problems—diabetes, heart disease, or other illnesses—which can threaten their

Norma McCorvey (left) stands with attorney Gloria Alfred in front of the Supreme Court building several years after *Roe* v. *Wade* was decided there. Because of McCorvey's actions, pregnant women in the United States have the right to choose whether or not to have an abortion—and all Americans have the right to pick a side of the issue.

life if they have a child. In these cases, abortion protects them. In addition, antiabortion laws discriminate against poor people. The rich always will be able to find a way to get an abortion; however, a poor woman may be driven to try an unsafe abortion or to perform one on herself. They also claim that laws against abortion take away a freedom in a supposedly free society. By taking away the right to have an abortion, say pro-choicers, government is not giving the woman a choice by telling her she must bear the child. However, if abortion is allowed, not only will women be free to choose, but every child born will be a wanted child.

Planned Parenthood also distributes literature about effective ways to prevent abortion. In its pamphlet, "Five Ways to Prevent Abortion (And One Way That Won't)," the group asks that contraception be made easily available, that sex education be provided to young people, and that men become more involved in sexual responsibility. They also ask for research dollars to help find new methods of birth control and Americans to adopt a more accepting attitude toward sexuality. If you are curious about the "one way that won't [prevent abortion]," this group says it is to make abortions illegal again. Then, they say, women will put themselves at risk with unsafe, illegal abortions done by unqualified practitioners.

Planned Parenthood is just one of the groups who is pro-choice. Who are these groups and what do they believe? Here is a sampling.

Catholics For A Free Choice represents those from the Roman Catholic Church who support the right to choose abortions. The group's main focus is to inform people that they can be Catholic *and* pro-choice. The group prints publications, including a quarterly news journal.

Choice began as a clergy consultation service. The group now makes available social and medical services, including abortion, to any individual, regardless of her ability to pay. Choice operates several hotlines to provide information and counseling for women deciding whether abortion is right for them. It also publishes directories of health services. Abortion is one of its focuses; the group also deals with other health issues.

The National Abortion Federation is geared toward people who perform abortions. The Federation maintains standards and guidelines for safe abortions in an effort to upgrade the quality of services offered. It also provides information on services offered throughout the United States. It publishes the "Consumer's Guide to Abortion Services" in English and Spanish.

The National Abortion and Reproductive Rights Action League has four hundred thousand members throughout the country, with forty-one state groups. The group is very active in politics. Members testify before Congress and at abortion hearings. They support pro-choice politicians for office. The group also produces educational materials to make Americans more aware of state and national laws regarding abortion.

The Planned Parenthood Federation of America has perhaps one of the largest staffs of any pro-choice or pro-life organization—10,068. This group operates nine hundred centers throughout the United States that provide educational and medical services for women. As part of its educational effort, Planned Parenthood provides contraception, as well as abortion and sterilization services. Through its efforts and services, Planned Parenthood informs women about sexuality and reproduction, so that they may make educated decisions.

The Pro-Choice Defense League provides a variety of workshops for the public on "reproductive rights." It also trains abortion clinic directors on how to deal with protestors, harassment, and violence.

Religious Coalition for Abortion Rights is made up of a variety of religious organizations that wish to protect a woman's right to choose abortion. The group serves as the coordinator for the messages from their members and distributes these messages in educational literature. A part of this group, the Women of Color Partnership Program, provides workshops and materials about access to health care, male responsibility, the church's role, and medical issues for women.

4

Parental Consent

Rebecca Bell was a beautiful seventeen-year-old who lived in Indiana.[1] A model student, she loved to play the flute. She loved her home and her family. She also loved animals and regularly went horseback riding. Everyone called her "Angel"—and she was an angel. Becky never did anything wrong . . . never even got a spanking. Nobody worried about Becky. She always did everything she should—until she met her boyfriend.

He was a friend of the family—the only boy she ever dated. She just loved him! He was a rebel. He loved hot cars, wild music, and drugs. Still, Becky thought her boyfriend was wonderful.

Becky had just turned seventeen when she found out she was pregnant. She immediately went to tell her boyfriend. She didn't expect the response he gave her.

"Get . . . out of my life," he said cold-heartedly. "I don't want you. I used you." Becky didn't know what to do. She didn't want her parents to know. So she went to the local Planned Parenthood about two miles from home. The counselor asked her age and Becky replied. Then the counselor told Becky, in Indiana, a girl cannot have an abortion if she is under eighteen without one of her parents approving.

This state law is called parental consent. Some states require it; others require that parents be notified. Some states do not require parents to know at all. Of course, this is constantly changing as laws are revised. (See Appendix for a listing of all states.)

Becky was upset when she heard her parents were required to know. She was not afraid of her parents. She loved them more than life. Becky was ashamed. She didn't want to shame the family. She didn't want to hurt them.

She told the counselor, "I can't tell them and I won't." So the counselor suggested the only other option, allowed by some states, including Indiana. Becky could go to the judge and try to get a bypass.[2] This is when a girl goes before a judge instead of her parents, and the judge helps her to decide what to do. The judge decides whether she is mature enough to make the decision of getting an abortion. If the judge does not find her mature, a decision is made as to whether the abortion is the right thing for her. During this process, the teenager has to confide her sexual life to as many as twenty-three people.[3] Also, if a judge is

Rebecca Bell discovered that she was pregnant when she was seventeen years old.

strongly pro-life, he or she may not grant an abortion, even when convincing evidence is presented.[4]

Becky said simply, "How can I tell a judge when I can't even tell my mom and dad? I can't."

Becky's last choice was Kentucky, 110 miles from home. There, she didn't need parental consent to get an abortion. That's what she was going to do, even though she had never even been out of Indianapolis. Since Becky had just gotten her driver's license she would be able to drive herself. She didn't know it, but about one hundred thousand women each year travel to another state in order to get an abortion because of parental consent laws.[5]

Becky's family was planning their annual vacation to Florida. For the first time, Becky told her parents that she did not want to go. She did not tell them she was going to make a trip to Kentucky instead. Her mother noticed Becky was sad and reading all the time. She thought, "What is wrong with my daughter?" Becky's parents thought the trip to Florida—time away with the family—was exactly what she needed to get her spirits back. So, they made her go. Becky stopped planning her trip to Kentucky.

When they came home from Florida, Becky asked her mother if she could go to a party on the south side of town. "My God," her mother said. "I'm not going to let you go to a party on the south side of town." But Becky's older brother Billy stood up for her. "Oh, Mom, please let her go. You protect Becky. Let her do something." To which Becky added, "Mom, a friend of mine's in trouble and I want to spend the night, maybe." Becky's mother knew something was wrong. Reluctantly, she agreed to let Becky go to the party.

Later that night, close to one o'clock in the morning, Becky knocked on the front door of her house, something she never did. Her mother opened the door, took one look at her and said, "Oh my God, Beck, what's wrong?" And Becky replied, "Oh, Mom, it was a horrible party. I feel like somebody put something in my Coke." She was crying. Becky asked if she could just go to bed. Her mother did not know it, but Becky had had an illegal abortion.

The next day, Becky woke up sick with a stiff neck. As usual, she went to work at Cubb Food as a cashier, but she just barely made it through the day. She came home, studied, and went to school on Monday. At school, she was sick all day, and laid her head down on her desk. She did not eat. Becky was getting weak. That night, she told her mother she had the flu like her dad. Her mother believed her.

By Wednesday, Becky had a fever and a strange cough. She lay there pale and shivering. Her mother insisted Becky go to a doctor. But Becky pleaded with her mother. "Oh, Mom. Oh please, please don't make me." All the time, she was thinking her menstrual period hadn't started, and so the abortion had not yet been completed. She knew if she went to the doctor he would know and tell her parents. So she just refused to go.

On Friday at 11 A.M., Becky got her period. She sat up on the couch, where she'd been all week, and said, "Mommy, I'll go to the doctor now." She was smiling. She thought she was free and clear and no one would ever know.

Becky's mother quickly got her husband, Bill. "We've got to get Beck to the hospital." When Becky tried to stand up to go, she just kind of fell backwards. Her parents thought she was just weak and that she would be okay. In fact, Becky was dying.

On the way to the hospital, Becky laid her head on her mother's lap. When they arrived, the nurses examined Becky and said, "What have you done to yourself?" Becky's mother was confused. "What are people talking about?" she thought. "Becky's got pneumonia or flu . . . she's going to be okay." But when the nurses tried to draw blood, they couldn't. Becky's veins had collapsed.

They put Becky in the pediatric ward. They asked her parents to go talk to her, telling them there was something really wrong but they didn't know what. Becky's mother leaned down and said, "Talk to me honey. Tell Mommy what's wrong." And Becky took her little love knot ring off and handed it to her mother. "Mommy," she said. "Forgive me for what I've done." And then, she seemed to die.

The hospital staff rushed Becky onto life support. They told her parents, "We don't know if we can save the baby." Becky's mother was shocked. "What baby? I don't want any baby, I want my child!" But they could not save Becky. Rebecca Suzanne Bell died on September 16, 1988. "The whole family died when she did," said Becky's mother.

The staff did an autopsy because what had happened was so odd. Becky died within twenty-four hours of being admitted to the hospital, and by law they had to investigate. They called Becky's parents after the autopsy to tell them, "Your Rebecca Suzanne has died from an illegal, botched abortion." "Not my girl," said her father, Bill. "Not my Becky." But it was true.

Becky's mother, Karen, wanted to lie about the cause of Becky's death. They lived in a small town, where everybody knows everybody and they talk. She wanted to lie and say Becky died of pneumonia, so no one would say she was a bad girl. Her husband and son agreed.

There were hundreds of people at the funeral. The minister came over just as it was starting. He said, "I know what you're going to want me to say, but you should tell the truth so you can hold your head up in the community." He continued, "I know how Becky died." The Bells agreed. Karen Bell bowed her head so she did not have to look at people. When it was all over, everyone was in shock. Billy took a hold of his mom's and dad's hands and asked if he could close the casket. He went over and patted his sister on the head. "Becky, nobody will ever hurt you again," he said.

Becky's family found out the full story after the funeral. It took months of talking to friends and Planned Parenthood counselors to piece it together. It was months later when the Bells found out about the parental consent law.

Parental consent laws get support from both sides of the abortion issue—pro-life and pro-choice—and especially from parents. A national poll taken for Cable News Network and *Time* magazine in May 1990 found only 38 percent of the people surveyed said teenagers should be able to have an abortion without their parents' permission. Fifty percent felt *both* parents should be involved.[6]

People who support the laws—pro-choice and pro-life alike—say teenagers are too immature to make such a

Due to complications caused by an illegal abortion, Rebecca Suzanne
Bell, born August 24, 1971, died September 16, 1988.

big decision on their own. They need their parents to help them. They believe the law encourages communication.[7]

People who are against parental consent say the laws are well-intended, but in some cases may cause teenagers to find illegal abortions or become abused by family members. They believe teenagers are mature enough to handle a decision about abortion. They feel this law is another way of stopping abortions.[8]

The Center for Population Options says that, in spite of the parental consent laws, more than 60 percent of teenagers tell their parents about their pregnancy anyway. In fact, 74 percent of teens under age fifteen voluntarily told a parent and 80 percent of teenagers under sixteen came to an abortion clinic with their mothers.[9] One teenage girl put it this way, "I don't think a person should have to, but I really think they should [talk to their parents]. I really think it's in the best interest of everyone. But I think [the laws are] wrong. . . ."[10]

Says Becky's mom, Karen:

> We didn't know about parental consent. We didn't know what she went through and that's what killed us. I was always home, and that's why I never thought anything would happen to my girl, or to my son, because I was there. But that's what you really have to worry about—the daughters who love you more than life, like Becky loved us. She didn't want to disappoint us, and wouldn't disappoint us and would not do what the law said for anything. I think it's the stupidest law in the world, but I would have voted for it![11]

On the other side of the issue, the following story appeared in the November issue of *AUL Insights*, published by Americans United for Life. It is reprinted with permission.[12]

The Case for Parental Consent

Becky Bell's parents aren't the only ones who hold a strong opinion about laws that involve parents in a teenager's abortion decision. While Karen and William Bell travel around the country testifying against parental consent legislation, a California mother wishes the law had safeguarded her rights and those of her teenage daughter.

At a small junior high school in rural California, Virginia Preston met with her daughter's principal early in 1985. She asked him to inform her of anything that related to fourteen-year-old Erin, who had a learning disability. He agreed, and they instituted a program of written daily reports from Erin's teachers.

After a sex education class in March, Erin told her homeroom teacher that she thought she might be pregnant. The teacher and a colleague explained to Erin that she must act quickly to get an abortion and that she didn't have to tell her parents of the suspected pregnancy. The teacher sent a note to Mrs. Preston saying that Erin needed to stay after school, but instead drove the girl to a health center for a pregnancy test. The results were positive.

The teacher and her colleague then met to discuss how they would procure an abortion for Erin. Both the principal and school superintendent allegedly were aware of Erin's pregnancy and her teacher's involvement, and neither notified the girl's parents.

Erin was taken to the welfare department where the teacher helped her apply for MediCal benefits to pay for the abortion. That day she forged Erin's daily reports so that Mrs. Preston would think her daughter had attended regular classes.

On March 22, during school hours, a rape crisis counselor took Erin to an abortion clinic for pre-abortion testing. Staff members didn't attempt to determine her level of maturity or understanding, but told her abortion was quick and easy and that her parents need never know about it.

On Friday, Erin's teacher sent a note home with her, asking if the teenager could babysit the next day. She explained that she would be out late and requested that Erin stay overnight at her home. But Erin didn't babysit. Instead, she was taken to Chico Feminist Women's Health Center for an abortion.

Erin kept quiet about the abortion. But four days later, Mrs. Preston received a telephone call from the school nurse, who told her for the first time about Erin's abortion and its resulting complications. Erin was rushed to a hospital for emergency surgery.

The Prestons were angry, and rightly so. They had asked to be kept informed of their daughter's progress and concerns, but had been intentionally deceived. Erin and her mother filed suit against school and clinic officials. They charged that Mrs. Preston's constitutional right to rear her teenage daughter and Erin's constitutional "right to choose" had been disregarded since the people advising Erin had denied her any real choices.

Most of the school and clinic staff settled the case out of court. But the superintendent pressed for a decision, and a court ruled in his favor before the case went to trial. On August 7, 1990, the California Court of Appeals upheld the lower court's ruling, saying that "as a matter of law the various conduct alleged is not 'extreme and outrageous'" solely because California law permits minors to obtain abortions without the knowledge or consent of their parents. The California Supreme Court refused to hear the Prestons' appeal.

AUL attorney Ann-Louise Lohr, co-counsel in the case, remarked, "Here, an elaborate web of deception was spun by public officials, carried out in a clandestine [secretive] manner and perpetuated [sic] on an unknowing mother who was deceived and lied to in the name of 'assistance.' Such outrageous and deceptive conduct should not, as a matter of law, be tolerated."

The Right-to-Life View—Our Stories

Angel

Resting in my arms with my last name,
I will never call you bastard,
And you will never know that your father didn't
   love us enough.
Only twenty-four hours I have you,
But I cried and laughed enough to fill up both our
   lifetimes.
And often will I wonder and dream of invisible cribs.

—Jennifer (printed with permission) [1]

Jennifer was only nineteen when she became pregnant. She and her boyfriend were attending a Christian College in Pennsylvania. He was her true love—the first and only guy she ever slept with. They made love in January 1994, when she was on campus collecting her things to move back home. In February, she told her boyfriend she was pregnant.

"I felt really confused," said Jennifer. "But I felt much better when my boyfriend insisted I have the baby and give it up for adoption."

"I'll support you," he promised. He said he'd call Jennifer every single day they were apart. But he didn't. He didn't call for two months.

"I freaked out and got an abortion," confessed Jennifer. "I guess I panicked. Then, I told him I miscarried." Weeks later, Jennifer told him the truth. He was really mad.

Jennifer started taking birth control pills so it wouldn't happen again. But, that May, she found herself pregnant by the same boyfriend.

Jennifer's boyfriend was getting ready to move to North Carolina. When he heard about the second pregnancy, he asked if she wanted to move with him. Jennifer agreed.

She moved down to North Carolina on May 15. They lived together until Jennifer gave birth to a baby girl on January 27 and almost immediately gave her up for adoption. Then, she moved out February 10.

"At first, I was going to move out for one month, so we could have some space, but now it looks like it's going to be for a long time," said Jennifer. "We were constantly arguing throughout the whole pregnancy. I was really emotional. I would say, I can't deal with this, I'm going to have an abortion. No, I want to keep it. No, I want to give it up for adoption. My boyfriend didn't think he'd make a good father. He told me if I want to keep the baby, I can't live with him."

Giving up her daughter for adoption was one of the hardest things she has ever done—and what inspired the poem she wrote. Said Jennifer:

> The first month was really tough, because they give you thirty days to change your mind. My daughter was put in a foster home for thirty days, and I could see her anytime. I didn't want to see her, in case I'd change my mind and maybe make a mistake. So I ended up with less than twenty-four hours in the hospital with her.
>
> You have to be a really strong person emotionally to give a baby up for adoption. You also need strong people who are going to back you. Those strong people were my parents because they didn't tell me what they thought. They said it's up to me and they'll support my decision. When I finally did make the decision, my dad told me I made the right one.
>
> But it was really difficult. I receive pictures every month from my daughter's adoptive parents and that helps. I think they're planning—maybe at age four or five—whenever she can comprehend, to tell her she's adopted. Then I'll get to see her. So it's really not that bad.

In the fall, Jennifer returned to college to become a nurse, a lifelong dream of hers. She plans to specialize in obstetrics (childbirth). "I would love to work with babies," she said. In addition, she plans to pursue her poetry.

At seventeen, Gail Morgan is the mother of a baby girl—Sarah Marie.[2] She was sixteen when she got pregnant. She and her boyfriend had talked about that possibility, but they hadn't really expected it. Then one day Gail told her boyfriend her period was late. They hadn't taken proper precautions during sex. She and her boyfriend waited another two weeks—just in case Gail got her period.

They first broke the news to his mother because they thought she could handle it the best. She and Gail discussed the situation. "His mom was so supportive," said Gail. "She said she almost found herself in the same predicament and made me feel better."

After that, Gail and her boyfriend told his dad. "He was a little upset for maybe the first week but after that he supported us the whole time," said Gail.

That same night, Gail told her mother, who later delivered the news to her husband. "My mom was very upset but she was glad I didn't want an abortion," explained Gail. Her voice took on a sad lilt. "My dad, however, just wanted me to get an abortion. And I didn't want that. My dad still hasn't really faced the fact it's happened yet."

Since Gail was thirteen, her father had said, if she ever got pregnant, he would kick her out of the house. So, when Gail realized she was pregnant, she began to make plans to live somewhere else. Her boyfriend's family agreed to let her move in with them. Gail's mother wanted Gail at home. But Gail's dad insisted she leave. He didn't kick her out on the streets, however. Instead, he found a maternity house where Gail could live. The house, called ABBA, provided home schooling and prenatal care.

A Portland, Oregon, family demonstrates in Buffalo, New York, on behalf of Operation Rescue, a pro-life group.

"It was really different [there]," said Gail. "My family is so close and then, living with strangers . . . well, I had to get used to a lot of different styles. I was there from July 11 until February 7, when I gave birth to Sarah Marie." As the fetus grew inside her, Gail became very excited she was having a baby.

Since giving birth, Gail has moved back in with her parents. "My mom's here for me," she says. "My dad's here for me, too, for emotional support, but he won't participate in anything financially. And my boyfriend's still with me."

Gail's typical day now starts around 8 A.M. when she gets up to feed and change the baby. Sarah Marie is awake for about an hour. Gail's breakfast is postponed until maybe 10:30 A.M. or 11 A.M. "That's one sacrifice [I have to make]," says Gail. After about an hour, Gail puts the baby downstairs in the playpen and attaches a heart monitor. "She's been having breath-holding episodes," explains Gail. Once the baby is comfortable, Gail gets something to eat. Often, she'll do her schoolwork as she eats. If she has enough time, she'll help her mother clean or do chores.

Gail puts the baby first before her own needs. "Today, she slept pretty well," said Gail, "but if she has a temper, I have to put the schoolwork off and take care of her." No sacrifice is too great. "Usually, I even wait to go to the bathroom until she's asleep, but today I had to take her because I couldn't hold it," Gail confessed.

"At night, the baby is up for as many as four hours, so I'm exhausted," she explains. "So usually I take just a little hour nap. And then after that, I get up and I clean some more. I'll do laundry, dishes, or something. Then, she'll wake up and I'll have to feed her again."

When asked what she would have been doing a year-and-a-half ago, Gail says she would have been wrapped up in boys. Her grades would have been dropping. "The crowd I was hanging out with," she explained, "was heading towards drugs." Having a baby just may have saved Gail from a similar fate. Her grades now are outstanding. She's almost done with tenth grade and will return in September to eleventh grade.

A very mature teenager, Gail spoke wisely about what she would say to other teenagers about this issue. Without hesitation, she said:

> Wait. I know everybody says that. I heard it before I had done it. But wait. The experience I'm having now is wonderful, but I would like to have my husband with me rather than my boyfriend. I'd rather he was able to enjoy with me everything I enjoy now. I mean, it's wonderful and it's very hard. It's a lot easier if you have someone with you.

Evie Roderer was older when she was faced with a similar decision.[3] "I was in my early twenties, living in Manhattan, and working as a ballroom dance instructor. I met a fellow who I really liked and I decided to move in with him. About a year later, I found out I was pregnant."

"It may sound strange but it was hard for me to connect being pregnant with a baby," she confesses. "I knew the eventual end of pregnancy was a big belly, and I thought it would be a problem because I was dancing. I didn't think of the baby at all. I thought of the more immediate circumstances." So Evie decided she would get an abortion, since abortions were legal.

The abortion clinic gave her a pregnancy test, and told her she was pregnant. Evie goes on:

> And they basically said to me 'when would you like to make the appointment?' They didn't ask me if I'd like to sit and think about it. They didn't describe to me what was going on in my body. They didn't sit down and talk to me about the possibilities of any other occurrences happening during the abortion or tell me there was nothing I should worry about. They didn't tell me anything other than well, when would you like to make the appointment?

Evie made the appointment and had the abortion. They put her to sleep. It was a relatively easy process for her at the time. That was pretty much the end of it.

Then, it happened again. She became pregnant by the same boyfriend about a year later. Again, she went to the abortion clinic. This time, she had told her parents about it. They had the same reaction as Evie did—that it was necessary to "remove" the problem. They never thought about the child. The second time, Evie found it a little harder, maybe because her father was there with her, or maybe because things were not good with her boyfriend. Or it could have been that, in the back of her mind, she was starting to think about the child.

Soon after, Evie moved back home. She met her husband-to-be a year or so later and eventually was married. "I was extremely blessed," said Evie, "after two abortions, I was able to conceive. I didn't have the physical problems a lot of women have."

When her son was born, Evie first realized what she had done. "After I gave birth, they brought him over to me. It was at that moment they handed me my baby, I realized, oh, my gosh, this is what I killed!" She described it as a wave of consciousness.

By this time, Evie had become a born-again Christian.

> With the love of God, knowing I have been forgiven for all my sins, including abortion, has eased a lot of it. I didn't have that terrible overwhelming guilt I know the majority of women experience and don't know what to do with. I had the remorse of not having my children. And that's what I have to live with daily.

There are moments when it is especially hard for Evie.

> A girl just told me a story two days ago about her sixteen-year-old daughter who was pregnant. Everybody gave her the money and they pushed her, telling her to go have the abortion. And she chose not to do it. Well, I know the little girl because she goes to my kids' school. She is the most beautiful little thing in the world. It's funny, at that moment, I had to hold back the tears about what I did, because my two children aren't here because of an abortion. So it's moments like that when you can't hold it back. It just floods through you and around you and over you. Right now, my children would have been about

As part of a pro-life presentation, Dr. Bernard Nathanson gave a copy of the antiabortion film *The Silent Scream* to the White House.

sixteen and seventeen. Now, I wind up speaking to a lot of teenage groups that age.

Like Evie, Laura* was also in her early twenties when she had her abortion.[4] Her experience at the clinic was much more frightening than Evie's, however. Laura became pregnant by her live-in boyfriend. They always used protection during sex. This time, they used a contraceptive sponge—and it failed.

Suspecting she might be pregnant, Laura went to her gynecologist. When she found out the pregnancy test was positive, Laura thought of her family and friends. What would they think? She couldn't ever tell them something like this.

The doctor noticed she was upset and handed Laura the name and number of a local doctor who performed abortions. Laura made an appointment. "I didn't know there were any other options," she said.

Laura's boyfriend came with her the day of the abortion. "I had to bring cash—no checks—and pay them up front," she remembers. Then, she and her boyfriend sat in the waiting room. She felt confused, very nervous, and emotional. She wondered if she was doing the right thing. The nurse gave her something, for cramping.

Laura then undressed and put on a gown. The nurse kept telling her to relax. Laura's boyfriend was allowed to stay with her and that helped somewhat. "They brought out the machine," said Laura. "I'll never forget that rumbly-sucking noise."

* Not her real name.

The doctor started the procedure and Laura doubled over. "It was so painful," she said, "beyond anything you can imagine . . . worse than childbirth! It was horrible. I was crying the whole time." Laura was squirming so much the doctor ordered two nurses to pin her down. Finally, it was over. The doctor told Laura the abortion was successful. She got dressed and stumbled out of the office.

Later at home, Laura sat on the couch crying. She kept praying, and saying over and over again, "I'm sorry. I'm sorry." Her boyfriend, too, was moved to tears.

Today, Laura is happily married to that boyfriend and they have children of their own. As for her experience, Laura accepts her "mistake" but vows she will never do it again. "I don't care what anyone says. I have to deal with it for the rest of my life. Not a day goes by that I don't think about the child I murdered."

Sara Smith was in her mother's womb when her mother tried to have an abortion.[5] The abortion was unsuccessful. As an abortion survivor, Sara has an important message for women of any age.

> My greatest concern is that a woman doesn't realize that when she exercises her "freedom of choice," and opts to end her unborn baby's life, she is removing the child's right to freedom of life. I firmly believe that most women who choose to abort aren't murderers, but rather that they are just ignorant of what they are really doing. That's why I try to target people who don't have a Christian background, who only hear the rhetoric and misinformation offered by Planned Parenthood and others. We did a TV

commercial and then did some fund-raising so that it could be shown on MTV. I would like to do more of that, but it is an expensive venture. Still, I meet with everyone I can to try to make sure the truth gets out. More than what I say, I want my life to be a testimony for those of us who are, in fact, abortion survivors. We are, after all, far more than just a "blob of flesh" to be examined on a petri dish. Just like the unborn babies we all once were, we are warm and alive and full of emotions and hopes and dreams. I [wish] were it in my power, that every child ever conceived could live to see the light of day, for we all have so much to offer the world. [6]

6

The Pro-Choice View—Our Stories

Fran was in her twenties and married when she considered abortion.[1] Her daughter, also named Fran, was five and her son was three. She and her husband finally had enough money to put a down payment on a house. This was a chance of a lifetime, but they needed Fran's salary to make the house payments.

"And I wound up being pregnant," said Fran. "If I had to stop working, we couldn't afford the house. It was either get an abortion or give up the dreams of the house. At the time, my marriage wasn't so great, and I decided at least I'd have the security of the house. My husband and I both talked about it. We decided jointly it was the thing for us to do. It was our only choice."

Fran and her husband went to Planned Parenthood. "They were very helpful. The counselors explained the whole procedure. Then, we had to come back. It wasn't like you were in there that day, you were 'bamboozled.' They gave me a physical, and made sure we knew our options. Then they scheduled it for us to come back, so we could have time to think about it," she explained.

Fran and her husband returned a few days later for the abortion. He was with her the whole time, except during the actual procedure. "It only takes a couple minutes," said Fran. "They tell you they will inject you. You'll feel a slight tingling sensation. It didn't even feel like a cramp. It was nothing. As a matter of fact, my periods are worse," she explained. "I didn't experience any pain or discomfort. I went home, walked around, was able to continue normally, do everything. I was up and about. I had two kids to take care of, after all."

Once the abortion was over, Fran felt a tremendous sense of relief. "Even now, I know I did the right thing," she said.

Based on her experience, she was able to counsel her daughter when she was facing a similar decision:

> I was open and frank with her when she told me she was pregnant. We sat down and talked about it. I told her I didn't think she was ready emotionally to handle it. She couldn't afford it. I told her if she planned to have the child, I would stick by her. But it would be her child. She would support it. She would take care of it. I would only be there if she needed me. Then I told her if she had an abortion, exactly the way it would feel. I made her think about it

before it happened, and I recommended that, but I told her it's her decision.

That's what I would recommend for teenage girls who find themselves in the same situation. Talk with your mothers if you can . . . or another adult. I don't mean to be sexist but I think you need to talk to a woman because you need to be put at ease. It's awkward enough talking to anyone about it.

Fran counsels runaways now. She tells them that when they are emotionally and financially secure, they can handle a child. Then it would be right for them to have that child:

> But I'm not really crazy about advising the girls to have the child and give it up for adoption, because sometimes they change their mind. It's easy to grow attached to your baby. I have a niece who was thirteen when she had a baby. She's raising it now, while she does drugs. So I think abortion is really the answer . . . If children are not truly wanted, they should not be brought into this world.

"Abortion's not for everyone," concludes Fran. "You have to be able to deal with it. But I feel if you think about it before you do it, you'll be able to handle it for the rest of your life. You'll have no regrets."

Jocelyn Edwards was a sophomore in college when she found out she was pregnant. Her story first appeared in *My Conscience Speaks, Catholic Women Discuss Their Abortions,* a series published by Catholics for a Free Choice in Washington, D.C. A portion of it is reprinted here, with permission.[2]

87

At Northwestern, if you start talking about babies and getting married, they take that [scholarship] money from you fast. I knew I couldn't afford Northwestern by myself, even with my parents helping, and school was wonderful. I had already been on the dean's list twice. Without that education, I knew I was not going to "get over." Today when I go on job interviews, people say, "You graduated from Northwestern? I was on the waiting list there. I didn't get in." That's how it works.

So if the baby came, the money went, along with my throat.

I got pregnant because my doctor told me to take a rest from the pill. The first month I stopped, I got pregnant, and that's why I'll probably keep taking them till I'm forty.

My periods are like clockwork and when one didn't come, I said, "Oh, God, what am I going to do now?" I went to church at Notre Dame and prayed that I wouldn't be pregnant. It didn't help me. I was still pregnant.

So I went over to the infirmary and cried. The doctor said, "Will you please stop crying, young lady." And he asked, "Are you on a scholarship?" I said, "Uh huh." "No wonder you're crying," he answered. Then he told me, "It's against my faith to tell any woman to get an abortion, but I would hate to see your life stopped because of a child."

I told him that I couldn't have a baby. He said, "All right. Come back tomorrow." So the next day I went back and he examined me to tell me exactly how many weeks pregnant I was. Then he explained the procedure that they do and told me how much money it would cost. He said that he would never tell anybody, that this was confidential and my parents would never know.

Pro-choice demonstrators stand on the steps of the Supreme Court.

The next day, he had to explain the whole thing again to my boyfriend John, who was very worried about me. John volunteered to get married. I refused because neither of us had finished school. And in my mind, I never wanted any dude to marry me because I was pregnant. I wanted him to marry me because he was in love with me. And I thought about those girls on welfare. My parents really worked to get me through school. I had another brother and sister who were gettting ready to come out of high school and go to college. My parents are very strong people, but they had all they could deal with. I was scared, but I knew that if I didn't have an abortion, I'd lose my mind . . .

John drove me to the clinic and I cried all the way. He kept saying, "You don't have to do this, Jocelyn." "Yes, I do. Yes I do," I cried.

The girls there were very nice to me. They explained the procedure, and talked about how you have to keep practicing birth control even on your breaks from the pill.

When I woke up from the procedure, I started screaming, "I can't see! I can't see!" I thought I had gone blind and God was punishing me. A doctor there handed me my contact lenses and said, "You can see just fine, Jocelyn."

I went home to sleep, got up the next day and went to class like nothing had happened. All I could think was, "Thank God it's over."

Catherine Dellabovi had two abortions. Her first was a horrible experience—an illegal abortion in 1960—done in an apartment by someone who wasn't qualified. Her second abortion was a legal one, performed in the mid-70s, after *Roe* v. *Wade* made abortion legal. She relates how much more comforting it was to have access to a legal abortion. Her story too appeared in *My Conscience Speaks, Catholic Women Discuss Their Abortions.* A portion of it is reprinted here, with permission.[3]

> I had no question in my mind but that there was going to be an abortion. I had the pregnancy test, and I made an appointment at a clinic. A friend went with me, a feminist who thought it was important for me to have some support. I went through the counseling and it was quite clear to the counselor that I had no questions in my mind. I had no deep desire to be a single mother.
>
> So, I had the abortion and the contrast between it and the illegal one was incredible, to have a real live doctor performing the abortion and not a Dr. Ann [the illegal abortionist who performed the previous one].
>
> I had a bit of difficulty in the recovery room, so I stayed a while. The wonderful part, the part that warmed my heart, if your heart can be warmed at such a time, was the sense of sisterhood among the women there. There were black women, white women, poor women and rich women. It was heartwarming how we would talk to each other.
>
> The notion that there were women together moving through this process and supporting each other was very important. Afterwards, I went home and rested, and went back to work the next day. The difference was rather incredible. The price, I think was $125, in contrast with the $400 illegal abortion many years before.

I subsequently have married and had a child. She's an absolute joy and I adore her. I'm enjoying the motherhood experience at age forty. In retrospect, the abortion decisions were the right decisions for me at the time. I think one of the worst things that could have happened to me would have been to marry this character in college. No one is ready for marriage at that age. Certainly, I was mature enough the second time—I was thirty-five—to know that that's not the way to have a child.

Whitney Caroll of Wichita, Kansas, tells her story from a slightly different viewpoint. (This story originally appeared as a letter to the editor in *Conscience*, the news journal of Catholics for a Free Choice, in Washington, D.C.).[4]

I have worked at a Planned Parenthood clinic for three years. In that time, I've met hundreds of women and heard many interesting, funny, shocking and sad stories. Recently I had a client whose story made me angry.

She had come in to see how far along her pregnancy was. The forms she had filled out indicated she was planning to continue the pregnancy. She was seventeen. When I called her back, she told me she really wanted to terminate, but because her boyfriend had been with her when she completed the paperwork, and he was thrilled about becoming a father, she couldn't be truthful on the forms. He too was seventeen.

When we met alone, she told me, she could not tell her parents about the pregnancy or her wish to terminate, because they were Catholic: she'd be condemned to hell. She had been too scared to act.

She had come to us, finally, to find out how far along she was, because the clinic she wanted to go to for a termination would not take her after sixteen weeks. After that, her only option would be Doctor George Tiller's clinic, and she was mortified to go there, because she had heard through church that he's a butcher, a murderer.

I asked her please not to believe everything she hears in church . . .

I assured her that Doctor Tiller is a medical doctor who operates a safe, professional, legal practice, and she need not be concerned about her safety. When our nurse practitioner examined her, it turned out that she was eighteen weeks into her pregnancy, and Doctor Tiller was her only option.

I shared with her our experience with a local Catholic high school that protests our clinics occasionally. They tell our clients that our birth control pills are fake because we want you to become pregnant so that you'll have an abortion. I wanted her to understand the outrageous, flat-out lies they use. It turned out that she attended this high school, and everyday it was drilled into students' heads that abortion is murder under any circumstances and that family planning services only encourage premarital sex. I applauded her for having the courage to think for herself and make her own choice.

So now—along with agonizing through this whole ordeal alone, because she could not go to her church or her family for support—since she waited so long, she'll have to undergo a two-day termination (including time for cervical dilation to allow removal or expulsion of a larger fetus), which increases her risk of complications if and when she plans a pregnancy in the future. Not to mention the great emotional and physical expense of a second-trimester abortion.

Anyone with basic comprehension skills— anyone in the church, schools, or legislature—can see in this story the crucial need for sex education (including abstinence), the need for family planning services, the need to be able to make our own decisions, for our own futures and our own bodies. In short, the need for freedom.

Wendy Botwin, too, works in an abortion clinic. As the head counselor in an inner-city clinic, she counsels teenagers and young women every day.[5] Says Wendy:

> I think it's a myth that everybody goes through this emotional trauma afterwards. For the most part, if people are very clear that's the decision they are going to make, they're real comfortable with making the choice. Usually people feel relieved afterwards and move on with their lives and are pretty happy.

Wendy provided some insight into the daily workings of an abortion clinic. There is no typical day, she said, but there are routines. Usually, abortions are done in the morning. But so much happens before the women are allowed to have an abortion:

> As a counselor, I review their medical history and decide whether the patient should be at our clinic, in a hospital, or elsewhere. Then, we do an ultrasound to determine how many weeks pregnant she is . . . . The ultrasound also alerts the clinic staff to other things, such as if the woman is carrying twins or she has cysts. . .

94

We start the counseling. Counseling involves rejection counseling. Sometimes a person is *not far enough* into their pregnancy, or *too far* into their pregnancy, to have an abortion and we have to tell them. A woman needs to be at least seven weeks pregnant to get an abortion. If it's too early, there's a greater chance of having an incomplete abortion or a missed abortion. Before seven weeks, the doctor can't even see the pregnancy. Also the cervix and uterus are really tiny before seven weeks, so it would be much easier to cause a perforation or cut.

Then, the counselors perform some social services, discussing money and family issues. "We help them figure out how they will pay for the service. We provide options counseling, going through a woman's individual situation and what choices make sense for her."

We spend enough time with someone to know if they are comfortable with their decision. With some people, it's clear they don't want to talk about it. Or they're absolutely sure and they don't need to talk about it. . . . We do not let anybody go through a procedure until both of us are absolutely sure that's what they want to do. We spend the time with people to make sure.

I don't care if people leave. . . . We're not trying to force anybody into anything. We're providing a service. If it's what they want, then we're there for them. If it's not what they want, then we can direct them and help them.

We actually explain the entire abortion procedure to our patients . . . unless they feel really uncomfortable and don't want to know it. We also

95

help them figure out what kind of anesthesia they're going to have: local, general, or twilight (a lighter dosage of general anesthesia which doesn't put people completely to sleep). Of course, we use only general anesthesia when people are twelve weeks pregnant and beyond. We spend a lot of time going over things they should expect and do or not do after the procedure.

In addition, the staff spends time educating people on birth control methods and what's best for them. They also direct the women to gynecological services.

At Wendy's clinic, all counseling is done individually or one-on-one, unless the child is under eighteen:

> With parental consent laws . . . I have to make sure the teenager's mother, father, or legal guardian is there to hear the counseling and consent to the actual abortion. We also meet separately with the teenagers to go over their medical history and their decision. But before the parental consent laws, many of the parents were there anyway. Now, because of the laws, the parents are forced to be there. The parents don't like it and the kids don't like it.

Once all counseling has been completed, the woman is scheduled for an abortion. If she is between sixteen and twenty weeks pregnant, she must come in twice. The first visit is once to have her cervix dilated with a sponge which stays in overnight. Then, she comes in the following day for the procedure:

> We see patients anywhere from eleven years old to fifty . . . The majority of the clinic's clientele are teenagers and people in their twenties. People have

Planned Parenthood supporters demonstrate for freedom of choice at a rally in Texas.

histories now. It's amazing the number of pregnancies an eighteen-year-old can walk in with already. There are eighteen-year-olds who have two kids, have had two abortions, and have had a miscarriage. This is not unusual. We see it a lot.

Wendy makes an interesting observation about the mix of people who enter her clinic. People who might be viewed as strongly pro-life use their services. "It's amazing, but more than half of the people we see are Catholic. I've even seen people who were, and maybe still are, protesters against abortion."

She tells a story of one patient who touched her life:

I saw a woman who was in her twenties who wanted an abortion. She had one or two kids already. The woman didn't have a job and was about to be kicked out of where she was living. When I told her she was too far along to get an abortion, the woman became suicidal. I think she was about twenty-five or twenty-six weeks pregnant. In other words, she just missed the legal deadline. I kept her in the clinic pretty much the rest of the day. She really wasn't able, or willing, to talk to me for a long time, but she still stayed. She ended up leaving with somebody at the end of the day. I knew she was a lot better when she left. I was supposed to have off work the next day, but I really wanted her to come back. I was scared for her. I knew she didn't get what she needed. So I tried to get her to come in the next day. And I came into work on my day off. But she never showed up. She ended up coming in the following day. I spent a lot of time with her, trying to figure out what she was going to do, and just being there for her. Months later, she called to tell me I was the only person she could really talk to. A year or so later, she called to thank me and tell me how things had really turned around for her. She ended up keeping her baby boy.

Wendy has advice for teenagers who may find themselves pregnant and alone and considering abortion:

> They need to know they're not the only one in their situation. I encourage kids, if they can't talk to their parents, to go to other places to get support. These places are private and confidential and no one has to know about it. Teenagers shouldn't be afraid to ask questions, even if they feel they're embarrassing or stupid questions. They shouldn't feel like they are making a bad choice if they decide to have an abortion.

Although Wendy's clinic services dozens of clients each day, it wasn't always easy for young women to get an abortion. Before *Roe* v. *Wade*, tales of back alley abortions were common.

Elaine Frederick, M.D., of San Francisco, California, tells this story:

> I wonder if young women today can fully identify with the situation only two decades ago. When I was a young doctor at a New York hospital, there would scarcely be a week go by when some woman wouldn't be brought to the emergency room near death from an illegal abortion. I saw some wonderful women die, and others reproductively crippled. Then, I too became pregnant, by accident, and though I was a doctor I could not ask any other doctor for help. In those days, if known, it would have cost us both our jobs. So I drove secretly to a Pennsylvania coal-mining town and was led to a secret location. I

was lucky. I wasn't injured. But I'm so glad that times have changed. I have five daughters and a son now. I hope they never have to make the agonizing decision about abortion, but if they do, I would hate for them to have to act like criminals and to risk their lives to do what they feel is right for their future.[6]

For Sherry Matulis of Peoria, Illinois, she sought an abortion because of rape:

I have been married for thirty-five years, I'm the mother of five children, grandmother of three. In the mid-fifties I was brutally raped and left for dead. I later discovered I was pregnant. I was horrified. I would not have that child. Our family doctor couldn't help. An abortion could have cost him and me twenty years in prison. I tried home remedies—like scalding myself, and falling down the stairs—but they didn't work. Finally, I found a local abortionist. I will always remember walking up those dark stairs. The incredible filth. The man had a whiskey glass in one hand and a knife in the other. The pain was the worst I have ever felt, but the humiliation was even worse. Hemorrhaging and hospitalization followed. I thought I would never be with my family again. I had no choice but I resent what I had to go through to terminate that pregnancy. And I resent the people who now say that women should be forced to endure such experiences.[7]

Where Do We Go from Here?

Do you remember Kiri from the first chapter of the book? She had to decide what her personal position on abortion would be. Here is what happened.[1]

After struggling with the decision all alone, Kiri decided to tell her parents. At first, as she predicted, they were upset. But they talked about the decision as a family. They, and Kiri, felt uncomfortable about abortion. However, her parents didn't think Kiri was ready to become a mother. The family decided it was best for Kiri to have the baby and then give it up for adoption.

So Kiri went to a maternity home, where she received counseling and continued her schoolwork. About two weeks after she turned seventeen, Kiri gave birth to a little girl. She was able to visit with her daughter in the hospital for about two weeks. She was even able to choose the adoptive parents. Kiri met them one day and handed over her baby girl. It nearly broke her heart.

Kiri never told the boy from the party about his daughter. She refused to list the father's name on the adoption papers. "What would I do if I saw him on the street?" Kiri often wondered. "Would I tell him?" If she ever did, he would be able to file for custody of their daughter—whom he hadn't agreed to put up for adoption. "I think he has a right to know he has a daughter," she says, "but I can never tell him."

Kiri still hears from the adoptive parents regularly and receives pictures of her daughter. "Those pictures were what got me out of bed each morning," she says. But she admits, although the parents are wonderful, it still hurts that she gave away her daughter.

Today, Kiri has a son. She became pregnant again around the time of her high school graduation—this time with a boyfriend whom she knew well and loved dearly. She thought he was the most wonderful person in the world, until she told him she was pregnant. He asked for a blood test to prove the baby was his, even though Kiri had been completely faithful to him. They argued extensively. Kiri's boyfriend wanted her to get an abortion. Having given birth once before, Kiri felt she couldn't do that. Eventually, Kiri and her boyfriend broke up because of their disagreement about the decision.

The second time around, Kiri's parents said she could raise the baby and live with them. She decided instead to move close by, and she talks with them all the time. Kiri's parents were upset she was giving up college:

> But I haven't given it up . . . I'm still going. It's just going to take a little longer to get the degree than I thought. I've got to be a mom, I've got to work, and I'm going back to school. I can never tell anyone it's easy because it's not. But I wouldn't trade my son for the world.

Says Kiri to teenagers who might find themselves in a similar situation:

> I think any choice to make when you're young and pregnant is difficult. But whatever you decide, it's got to be a personal decision, or you're going to resent the person who talked you into it.

She advises girls to consider how the decision might affect them in the future. "Think, in a few years, how am I going to be able to handle it? Is it going to make me feel good or rattle my conscience forever?" Of course, she concludes, "Not getting pregnant at all would be the best."

Kiri made the decision right for her. But, we are all different people. How can you make the *right* decision for you?

You have three responsible choices when you are pregnant: (1) continue the pregnancy, give birth, and keep the baby, (2) continue the pregnancy, give birth, and put the baby up for adoption, or (3) get an abortion.

If you are pregnant and decide to carry the baby, you probably will have many concerns. How will others react? Where will you live? What about school

A counselor talks with a young woman at the Planned Parenthood Clinic in the Bronx, New York.

and your plans for the future? Do you want to be a single parent or do you plan to marry? Do you want to keep the baby or give it up for adoption?

If you are considering abortion, you will face other concerns. Is permission from your parents required? Where will you get the money? Are abortions completely safe? Will you feel worse getting an abortion than having a baby?

Talking with others—such as in counseling—helps. Usually teenagers are afraid to admit to anyone else they are pregnant. But, it is important to talk with someone to work out your feelings and make an informed decision.

Your church, synagogue, or religious organization may be a resource. Priests, ministers, and rabbis often are good people with whom to talk. Or find an adult whom you trust and share your feelings. Your community also is a good source. Check the yellow pages of your phone book for local groups or clinics that offer counseling, or ask your school guidance counselor or nurse for a referral. There also are free national hot lines where you may speak with trained counselors.

However, be careful whom you choose as your counselor. A pro-life or pro-choice counselor will try to sway you to that side. It should be your personal decision. Remember what Kiri said. "It's got to be a personal decision, or you're going to resent the person who talked you into it."

Where to Go for Help

This book is just the starting point. Following are a selection of groups to contact for more information. These are not all of the groups in the United States, but merely a sample. You may find more groups in your local area. The groups listed in this book are organized in the two categories of pro-life and pro-choice. National, free hot line numbers are listed separately, at the end of each section, with their hours of operation.

PRO-LIFE GROUPS

ABBA Pregnancy Crisis Center
257 W. Broad
Palmyra, NJ 08065
(609) 829-0202

American Life League
P.O. Box 1350
Stratford, VA 22555
(703) 659-4171

Americans United for Life
343 S. Dearborn, Suite 1804
Chicago, IL 60604
(312) 786-9494

Feminists for Life
733 15th Street NW
Washington, DC
(202) 737-3352

Heartbeat International
1213 1/2 South James Rd.
Columbus, OH 43227-1801
(614) 239-9433
Provides directory of approximately three thousand pregnancy centers throughout the United States, which is free to libraries and a minimal cost for others.

Human Life International
7845 Airpark Rd., Suite E
Gaithersburg, MD 20879
(301) 670-7884

International Life Services, Inc.
2606 1/2 W. 8th St.
Los Angeles, CA 90057
(213) 382-2156

Liberty Godparent Home
1000 Villa Road
Lynchburg, VA 24503
(804) 384-3043
24-hour hot line number 1-800-542-4453
Offers housing, education, and medical care for pregnant teenagers free of charge.

Lutherans for Life
P.O. Box 819
10297 Congo Road
Benton, AR 72018
(501) 794-2212

National Christian Recovery HOPELINE
Last Harvest Ministries, Inc.
P.O. Box 462192
Garland, TX 75046-2192
(800) 422-4542

National Right to Life Committee
419 7th Street NW, Suite 500
Washington, DC 20004
(202) 626-8800

New Life Pregnancy Center
35 Garden Street
Mt. Holly, NJ
(609) 265-8222

People for Life
8154 N. 38th Street
Brown Deer, WI 53209
(414) 357-8584

Save A Baby
P.O. Box 101
Orinda, CA 94563
(415) 648-6436
(510) 758-1117

Sisters of Life
198 Hollywood Avenue
Bronx, NY 10465
(718) 863-2264

White Rose Institute
P.O. Box 5008
Hardy, AR 72542
(501) 856-2533

PRO-LIFE HOT LINES

Note to reader: Hot line numbers are not always based at the organization's address.

Bethany LifeLine
901 Eastern Avenue NE
Grand Rapids, MI 49503
1-800-BETHANY
Staffed 8 A.M–12 P.M., Eastern Time, seven days a week. Refers young women for free pregnancy testing and services, including adoption placement.

Birthright USA
National Office
P.O. Box 98363
(404) 451-6336
1-800-550-4900
Staffed twenty-four hours a day, seven days a week.

Christian Action Council
109 Carpenter Drive, Suite 100
Sterling, VA 20164
1-703-478-5661
Provides information and referrals.

National Life Center
686 North Broad Street
Woodbury, NJ 08096
1-800-848-LOVE
Staffed twenty-four hours a day, seven days a week.
Provides full line of free pregnancy services, including
maternity clothes, baby supplies, adoption referral,
financial aid; no minimum age requirement.

Pregnancy Center
1327 Dillon Heights Avenue
Baltimore, MD 21228
1-800-521-5530
Staffed twenty-four hours a day, seven days a week.
Provides pregnancy services through thirty-five hundred
centers located throughout the United States, including
career counseling; hot line staff will research answers to
any pregnancy-related questions.

PRO-CHOICE GROUPS

Abortion Rights Mobilization
175 Fifth Avenue, Ste. 814
New York, NY 10010
(212) 673-2040

Advocates for Youth
(formerly the Center for Population Options)
1025 Vermont Ave. NW, Ste. 200
Washington, D.C. 20005
(202) 347-5700

California Abortion and Reproductive
Rights Action League South
8455 Beverly Blvd., #303
Los Angeles, CA 90048
(213) 951-1160

Catholics for a Free Choice
1436 U St. NW, No. 301
Washington, DC 20009
(202) 986-6093

Committee to Defend Reproductive Rights
25 Taylor Street, Ste. 704
San Francisco, CA 94102
(415) 441-4434

Family Health International
P.O. Box 13950
Research Triangle Park, NC 27709
(919) 544-7040

The Feminist Majority Foundation
8105 W. Third Avenue, Ste. 1
Los Angeles, CA 90048
(213) 651-0495

HiTops
21 Wiggins Street
Princeton, NJ 08540
(609) 683-5155

National Abortion and Reproductive
Rights Action League (NARAL)
1156 15th Street NW, Ste. 700
Washington, D.C. 20005
(202) 973-3000

Planned Parenthood Federation of America
810 Seventh Avenue
New York, NY 10019
(212) 541-7800

Religious Coalition for Reproductive Choice
1025 Vermont Avenue NW, Ste. 1130
Washington, DC 20005
(202) 628-7700

Right to Choose Education Fund
P.O. Box 343
East Brunswick, NJ 08816
(908) 254-8665

PRO-CHOICE HOT LINES

Choice
1233 Locust St., Floor 3
Philadelphia, PA 19107
(215) 985-3355
Hot line, 1-800-84-TEENS
*Staffed Tuesday, Wednesday, and Thursday
from 7 A.M.–9 P.M.*

National Abortion Federation
1436 U Street NW, Ste. 103
Washington, D.C. 20009
(202) 667-5881
*Confidential Hot line for abortion information,
counseling, and referrals 1-800-772-9100
(operated 9:30 A.M.–5:30 P.M. Eastern Time)*

OTHER

**National Organization on Adolescent
Pregnancy, Parenting, and Prevention**
4421A East-West Highway
Bethesda, MD 20814
(301) 913-0378
NOAPPP has no position on abortion.

Appendix

Following is a summary of state parental involvement laws. However, laws in each state change daily. For the most up-to-date information in your state, contact your state legislature.

This chart is excerpted from "State Parental-Involvement Statutes" (August 1994), copyright 1995, Americans United for Life, 343 S. Dearborn Street, Ste. 1804, Chicago, IL 60604. Used by permission.

State	Requirement	Number of Parents	Judicial Bypass
AL	consent	one	yes
AK	consent	one	no
AZ	consent	one	yes
AR	notice	one	yes
CA	consent	one	yes
CO	consent	one	no
CT	no law	no law	no law
DE	notice	one	yes
DC	no law	no law	no law
FL	no law	no law	no law
GA	notice	one	yes
HI	no law	no law	no law
ID	notice	two	no
IL	notice	one	yes

State	Requirement	Number of Parents	Judicial Bypass
IN	written consent	one	yes
IA	no law	no law	no law
KS	notice	one	yes
KY	written consent	one	yes
LA	consent	one	yes
ME	other*	one	yes
MD	notice	one	no
MA	written consent	two	yes
MI	consent	one	yes
MN	notice	two	yes
MS	written consent	two	yes
MO	written consent	one	yes
MT	notice	one	yes
NB	notice	one	yes
NV	notice	one	yes
NH	no law	no law	no law
NJ	no law	no law	no law
NM	consent	one	no
NY	no law	no law	no law
NC	consent	one	yes
ND	written consent	two	yes
OH	notice	one	yes
OK	no law	no law	no law
OR	no law	no law	no law
PA	consent	one	yes

State	Requirement	Number of Parents	Judicial Bypass
RI	consent	one	yes
SC	consent	one (or grandparent)	yes
SD	notice	one	no
TN	consent	one	yes
TX	no law	no law	no law
UT	notice	two	no
VT	no law	no law	no law
VA	no law	no law	no law
WA	no law	no law	no law
WV	notice	one	yes
WI	other**	one	yes
WY	written notice and consent	one	yes

*Maine requires one adult family member or one parent 24-hour notice unless counseled by a physician.

**Wisconsin reequires consent from one parent or adult family member.

Chapter Notes

Chapter 1

1. Personal interview with Kiri, March 1995. (Real name withheld to protect her identity.)

Chapter 2

1. *Merriam-Webster's Collegiate Dictionary,* 10th edition, (1993), p. 3.

2. *Women Who Have Abortions, The Truth About Abortion,* A Fact Sheet Series from the National Abortion Federation, Washington, D.C., February 1992, p. 1.

3. Written comments of Jon Knowles, Director of Sexual Health Information, Planned Parenthood Federation of America™, August 30, 1995.

4. Robert Boyd, Alissa Rubin, Marty Westman, and George Rorick, "Abortion: An Issue that Divides Us, Beyond the Rhetoric"; "Medicine," Knight-Ridder Tribune newswire printed in *The Boca Raton News* (Florida), October 14, 1990, p. 1F.

5. Written comments of Jon Knowles, Director of Sexual Health Information, Planned Parenthood Federation of America™, August 30, 1995.

6. *What Is Abortion?, The Truth About Abortion,* A Fact Sheet Series from the National Abortion Federation, Washington, D.C., February 1992, pp. 1–2.

7. *Women Who Have Had Abortions, The Truth About Abortion,* A Fact Sheet Series from the National Abortion Federation, Washington, D.C., October 1990, p. 1.

8. Bea Armstrong, "Abortion By Prescription," *Detroit Free Press*, April 3, 1990, p. F1.

9. *Facts on RU 486,* fact sheet, Right to Choose Education Fund, East Brunswick, N.J., September 1993, p. 1.

10. Laura Fraser, "A Chemical Solution?" *Vogue*, October 1994, pp. 372–373, 420–421.

11. Ibid.

12. Personal interview with Wendy Botwin, March 1995.

13. *Women Who Have Abortions*, October 1990, p. 1.

14. Ibid.

15. Ibid.

16. *Parental Consent and Notification Laws,* fact sheet, Right to Choose Education Fund, East Brunswick, N.J., October 1990, p. 1.

17. Charles C. Clark, "Teenagers and Abortion, State Laws Requiring Parental Involvement Stir Opposition," *CQ Researcher*, Vol. 1, No. 9, July 5, 1991, p. 443.

18. Gary Turbak, "When Children Have Children," *Kiwanis Magazine*, May 1991, p.

19. Ibid.

20. Ibid.

21. Clark, p. 441.

22. Turbak, p. 50.

23. Ibid., p. 21.

24. Ibid.

25. "Too Soon, Too Sorry," *People*, October 24, 1994, p. 52.

Chapter 3

1. Marian Faux, *Roe v. Wade, The Untold Story of the Landmark Supreme Court Decision That Made Abortion Legal,* (New York: Macmillan Publishing Company, 1988), pp. 4–6.

2. Ibid.

3. Ibid., pp. 10–24.

4. *The Medical History of Abortion*, fact sheet, Right to Choose Education Fund, East Brunswick, N.J., October 1990, p. 1.

5. Robert Boyd, Alissa Rubin, Marty Westman and George Rorick, "Abortion: An Issue that Divides Us, Beyond the Rhetoric;" section titled "History," Knight-Ridder Tribune newswire printed in *The Boca Raton News* (Florida), October 14, 1990, p. 1F.

6. *The Medical History of Abortion*, p. 1.

7. Ibid.

8. Ibid.

9. *Most Religious Americans Are Pro-Choice*, fact sheet, Religious Coalition for Reproductive Choice, Washington, D.C., December 1994, p. 1.

10. Ibid.

11. Boyd, Rubin, Westman, and Rorick, p. 1F.

12. Ibid.

13. *The Voice of our Foremothers, Pro-Life Feminism*, brochure, Feminists for Life of America, Washington, D.C. (no recorded date), p. 2.

14. Faux, p. 167.

15. Maureen Harrison and Steve Gilbert, *Landmark Decisions of the United States Supreme Court*, (Calif.: Excellent Books, 1991), p.119.

16. Boyd, Rubin, Westman, and Rorick, p. 1F.

17. Landes, Siegel, and Foster, p. 9.

18. Ibid., p. 10

19. Ibid., p. 12

20. Cynthia Gorney, "Getting an Abortion in the Heartland, For Pro-Choice Women in South Dakota, There's Only One Choice," *Washington Post National Weekly Edition*, October 15–21, 1990, pp. 10–11.

21. Sonya Ross, "Abortion Foes Picket CNN Headquarters Over Documentary," *Associated Press Wire*, July 14, 1989, p. 1.

22. Sara Rimer, "Brookline Shows Fervor In Keeping Clinics Open," *The New York Times*, January 3, 1995, p. A12.

23. *U.S. Supreme Court Decisions on Abortion*, fact sheet, Right to Choose Education Fund, East Brunswick, N.J., July 1994, p. 4.

24. Robert Furlow, "Abortion Rally Offers Other Side of 'Silent Scream,'" *Associated Press Wire*, May 22, 1985, p. 1.

25. Stephen J. Hedges, David Bowermaster, and Susan Headden, "Abortion: Who's Behind the Violence?" *U.S. News & World Report*, November 14, 1994, p. 50.

26. Mireya Navarro, "Abortion Foe Is Guilty of Murder in Deaths of 2 at a Florida Clinic," *The New York Times*, November 3, 1994, p. A1.

27. Bill Kaczor, "Escorts Girding for Demonstrations at Pensacola Clinic," *Associated Press Wire*, August 5, 1994, p. 1.

28. Gustav Niebuhr, "Anti-Abortion Tactics Debated By Nation's Christian Leaders," *The New York Times*, January 9, 1995, A. 1.

29. Niebuhr, p. A1.

30. Personal interview with Lindsay, September 1995. (Real name withheld to protect her identity.)

31. "Special Issue on Repeat Abortion," *Association for Interdisciplinary Research in Values and Social Change Newsletter*, Volume 2, No. 3, Summer 1989, p. 1.

32. Monte Harris Liebman, M.D., "What is Wrong with Abortion?," fact sheet (no recorded date), p. 1.

33. *Everyone's Biography*, Human Life International, fact card (no recorded date), p. 1.

34. *Significant Events in a New Life*, American Life League, Inc., fact sheet (no recorded date), p. 1.

35. *The First Nine Months,* Focus on the Family brochure, October 1993, p. 10.

36. *Every Child Deserves the Right to be Born,* Americans United for Life brochure, 1992, p. 1.

37. *Abortion: What about . . . Rape? Incest?,* Lutherans for Life brochure, 1990, p. 2.

38. *Abortion: The Hard Cases,* NRL Educational Trust Fund, October 1991, p. 3.

39. Ibid., pp. 1–3.

40. Ibid., p. 6.

41. Boyd, Rubin, Westman, and Rorick, p. 1F.

42. Ibid.

43. Ibid.

44. Ibid.

45. Marjorie Reiley Maguire and Daniel C. Maguire, "A Guide to Making Ethical Choices," Catholics for a Free Choice, 1983, p. 1.

46. *Safety of Abortion, The Truth About Abortion,* A Fact Sheet Series from the National Abortion Federation, Washington, D.C., April 1990, p. 1.

47. *Abortion Arguments,* Right to Choose Education Fund, East Brunswick, N.J., December 1993, p. 1.

48. *Safety of Abortion,* April 1990, p. 1.

49. *Ten Facts on Abortion,* Right to Choose Education Fund, East Brunswick, N.J., August 1992, p. 1.

50. Ibid.

51. *Psychological Studies on Abortion,* Right to Choose Education Fund, East Brunswick, N.J., December 1993, p. 1.

52. *Women Who Have Abortions, The Truth About Abortion,* A Fact Sheet Series from the National Abortion Federation, Washington, D.C., October 1990, p. 2.

Chapter 4

1. Personal interview with Karen Bell, February 1995.

2. Charles S. Clark, "Teenagers and Abortion, State Laws Requiring Parental Involvement Stir Opposition," *CQ Researcher*, Vol. 1, No. 9, July 5, 1991, p. 453.

3. Ibid.

4. Susan Flinn, "Adolescent Abortion and Mandated Parental Involvement: The Impact of Back Alley Laws on Young Women," The Center for Population Options, brochure, 1993, p. 4.

5. Barbara Brotman, "The Abortion Maze: Crazy Quilt of Laws Among States Likely to Get Even Worse," *Chicago Tribune*, January 14, 1990, p. 11.

6. Clark, p. 458.

7. Ibid.

8. Ibid.

9. Flinn, p. 3.

10. Rebecca Stone and Cynthia Waszak, "Adolescent Knowledge and Attitudes About Abortion," *Family Planning Perspectives*, Volume 24, No. 2, March/April 1992, p. 55.

11. Personal interview with Karen Bell, February 1995.

12. Melodie Schlenker Gage, "A Mother Fights for Her Rights," *AUL Insights*, (Americans United for Life: Chicago), November 1990.

Chapter 5

1. Personal interview with Jennifer, March 1995. (Real name withheld to protect her identity.)

2. Personal interview with Gail Morgan, March 1995.

3. Personal interview with Evie Roderer, March 1995.

4. Personal interview with Laura, March 1995. (Real name withheld to protect her identity.)

5. Floyd Allen, "Sarah Smith: 'I'm the half of me that lived'," *Celebrate Life*, Volume 17, No. 1 (January–February 1995), p. 12.

6. Ibid., p. 11.

Chapter 6

1. Personal interview with Fran, March 1995. (Last name withheld to protect her identity.)

2. Constance McKenna, Karen Johnson, and Marjorie C. McKenna, *My Conscience Speaks, Catholic Women Discuss Their Abortions*, (Catholics For A Free Choice: Washington, D.C., 1981), pp. 3–5.

3. Ibid., pp. 29–32.

4. Whitney Carroll, "The Makings of a 2nd Trimester Abortion," *Conscience*, a News journal of Pro-choice Catholic Opinion, Spring/Summer 1995, p. 60.

5. Personal interview with Wendy Botwin, March 1995.

6. *Nine Reasons Why Abortions Are Legal*, Planned Parenthood Federation of America, Inc., New York, April 1990, p. 4.

7. Ibid., p. 7.

Chapter 7

1. Personal interview with Kiri, March 1995. (Real name withheld to protect her identity.)

Bibliography

Boyd, Robert, Alissa Rubin, Marty Westman, and George Rorick. "Abortion: An Issue that Divides Us, Beyond the Rhetoric." Knight-Ridder Tribune newswire printed in *The Boca Raton News* (Florida), (October 14, 1990),

Clark, Charles C. "Teenagers and Abortion, State Laws Requiring Parental Involvement Stir Opposition." CQ Researcher, *Congressional Quarterly, Inc.*, July 5, 1991,

Faux, Marian. *Roe v. Wade, The Untold Story of the Landmark Supreme Court Decision That Made Abortion Legal.* New York: Macmillan Publishing Company, 1978.

Fraser, Laura. "A Chemical Solution." *Vogue*, (October 1994).

Herda, D. J. *Roe v. Wade, The Abortion Question,* Hillside, N.J.: Enslow Publishers, Inc., 1994.

Landes, B.A., Alison, Mark A. Siegel, Ph.D., and Carol D. Foster, B.A., M.L.S. *The Information Series on Current Topics: Abortion, An Eternal Social and Moral Issue.* Wylie, Tex.: Information Plus, 1994 Edition.

Stone, Rebecca and Cynthia Waszak. "Adolescent Knowledge and Attitudes About Abortion." *Family Planning Perspectives*, Volume 24, No. 2, (March/April 1992).

"Too Soon, Too Sorry." *People*, (October 24, 1994).

Turbak, Gary. "When Children Have Children," *Kiwanis*, (May 1991).

Index